Helping Children Write Simple Science Reports

The most successful writing experiences for children have one thing in common - adequate time has been spent at the prewriting stage. During the prewriting stage motivation is established, background knowledge is developed, and requirements of the writing assignment are clarified. During this time, the writing process is modeled. Don't rush through this step.

Establishing Purpose

Your students need to know the reason they are doing a specific writing assignment. Explain why they have been given the assignment and what you will be looking for in the finished project:

- Are they writing to show what they have learned through class study on a topic?
- Are they writing to show what they have learned doing their own research?
- Are they writing to show how well they can write a specific type of report?
- Will you be looking primarily at content?
- Are you looking for how well they use the mechanics of written language?

State your purpose in clear, easily understood language. "You are going to write a short report about _(topic)_. You need to include these three points...." "You are going to write a description of _(topic)_. Describe its size, color, what it is made of, what it can do,...."

Provide Background Information

If the whole class is working on the same topic, share information by reading books together and viewing videos, filmstrips, etc., to develop background knowledge before they begin to write. Discuss what they have learned and make notes on the chalkboard for students to use as a reference.

If students are going to be writing on different topics, set up a research area containing books, magazines, filmstrips, etc., they can use in doing their own research. Arrange with the librarian for times when students can do further research in the library. Be sure your students have had some group experience in doing research and making notes before you expect independent reports.

Modeling the Process

Use these steps for writing a simple science report with the whole class:

1. Select one topic from the book.

2. Read one or more selections about the topic to your class.

3. Brainstorm with the class to create a list of facts they learned from what you read. List the facts on the chalkboard or a chart for students to use as a reference source.

4. Group facts about a particular aspect together.

5. Have children write a short report using these facts. (With less-able groups of students or students who have never written a report before, you may wish to write the report together and have each student copy the report into their own books.)

These report forms can be used by:

• The Whole Class
The whole class can study and report on one specific animal or animal's home. Share many books and films about the topic with your class. Discuss physical characteristics, habits, habitat, and unusual adaptations of the animal or animal home.

• Cooperative-Learning Groups
Each group will select the animal or animal home it wishes to study. The students in the group are responsible for finding information about that animal. (Teacher can help by providing access to a variety of resources in class and opportunities to visit the library.) A record keeper for the group takes notes to be used in the final writing of the report.

• Individual Students
Each student will select an animal or animal home he/she wishes to study. The student is responsible for finding information about that animal. (Teacher can help by providing access to a variety of resources in class and opportunities to visit the library.)

Making Simple Science Report Booklets

Preparation of Materials

1. Reproduce the two pattern pages for each book topic. Color and cut out the patterns.

2. Cut writing paper in the same shape. Copy the proofed simple science report on this paper. If students are writing on the computer, format the page so that the text will fit in the required shape.

3. Provide a sheet of construction paper for the back cover. Cut to match the shape.

Putting Booklets Together

Put the pages in order as shown and staple together on the left-hand side.

Using Completed Reports and Stories

1. Present reports in special "author's chair" session. After authors read their reports, they can become science experts and answer questions about their topic.

2. Place the completed stories in your classroom library for everyone to read and share.

3. Place the books in your school library's "student-authored books" section.

4. Let each author share his/her book with a "reading buddy" in a lower grade.

5. Send the books home to be shared with the child's family.

Writing Stories

Any of the animals or animal homes in this book can be used as the starting point for writing a fiction story. Story starters are provided for each topic, but these are only suggestions. You and your students will be able to come up with funny or exciting titles of your own.

Young beginning writers need to be given the opportunity to write their "story" in as simple a manner as possible. These early experiences may be only a handful of sentences with a minimum of plot. This is a time where you just want them to be comfortable putting words to paper. Once this comfort level has been established, you can begin working on creating stories of more substance.

Prewriting

Have your students think about these questions as they plan their stories:

- **Who is this story about?**
- **When is it happening?**
- **Where is it happening?**
- **What is the problem of the story?**
- **How is the problem solved?**

Writing

Have students follow these steps:

1. Write a rough draft of their story.

2. Read the story to see if it says what they want it to say, to see if it makes sense, and to see if they want to make any changes in content.

3. Read the story to check mechanics and grammar.

4. Make a final copy.

5. Put the story into a cover and share with others.

Part I
Wild Animals

Contents

Simple Science Report

FROG

Provide books and other materials about frogs for students reporting on this animal. (You may need to read these to younger students.) Discuss the information they have learned, then assign a writing task.

Frogs by Peter Murray; Child's World, 1993
From Tadpole to Frog by Wendy Pfeffer; Harper Collins, 1994
A Frog's Body by Joanna Cole; Morrow Junior Books, 1980

Discussion Starters

How does a frog catch its food?

What does a frog eat?

Why are eyes on top of the head helpful to the frog?

How many different ways can a frog move?

Can you describe the life cycle of a frog?

Skeleton Discussion Starter

Look at the difference in the size of the bones in the front legs and the back legs of a frog. Why do you think this difference is necessary?

Writing Ideas

1. A Report about Frogs
   a. Tell what a frog looks like.
   b. Tell how a frog moves.
   c. Tell what frogs eat.
   d. Tell how frogs catch their food.

2. Describe how frogs have adapted to life in the water.

3. Write about the life cycle of a frog.

4. Write a story about a frog.

The Frog Who Forgot How to Hop
How to Catch a Frog
If I Were a Frog

Frogs

Frogs are amphibians. They live very near or in the water. Frogs lay clumps of jelly-like eggs in the water. The tadpoles that hatch out of these eggs do not look like frogs. They are all head and tail and breathe with gills. As time goes by the tadpole grows legs and lungs and the tail disappears.

A frog has big, round eyes placed on the very top of its head. The frog can peek out of the water without sticking its whole head above water. This helps keep the frog safe from hungry enemies.

A frog has four legs. Its back legs are large and strong. This makes the frog a great jumper. Its back feet are like flippers. This makes the frog a strong swimmer. The front legs on a frog are smaller than the back legs. The frog rests its front feet on the ground when it sits. Sometimes it uses the front feet like hands to push food into its mouth.

A frog sits and waits for its dinner to fly or crawl by. When an insect, snail, worm, small fish, or small snake gets too close to a hungry frog, it had better look out! The frog's long, sticky tongue reaches out and grabs the tasty creature. A frog's tongue is attached to the lower front of a frog's mouth. A frog has very tiny teeth in its upper jaw, but they are just used to help grip food so it doesn't escape.

Tree frogs live among grass and bushes, often away from water. They have little suction cups on their toes to help them climb. Many tree frogs in tropical countries are very bright colors.

 Simple Science Reports

Frog Pattern

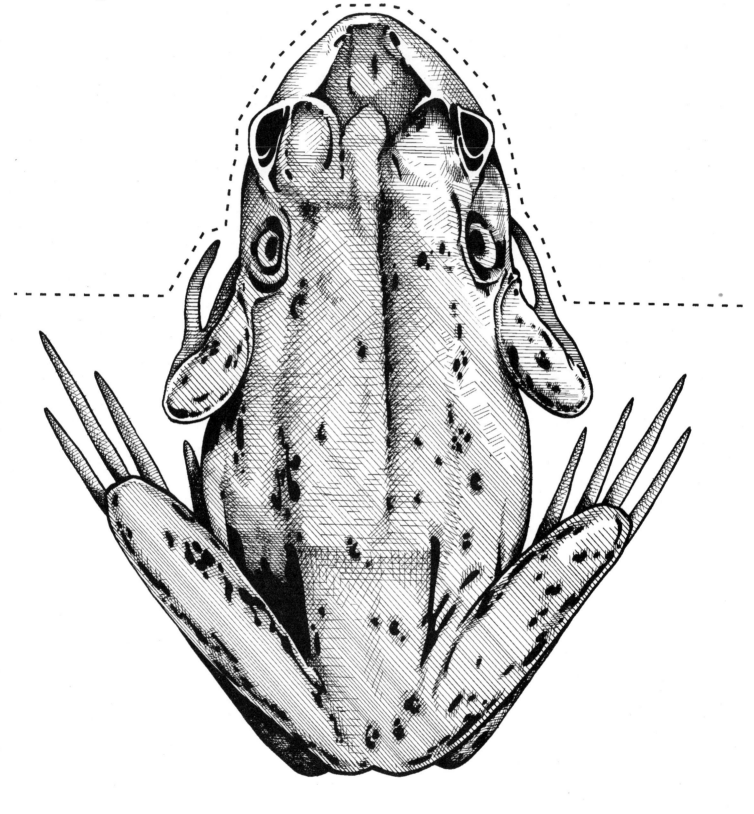

Frog Skeleton

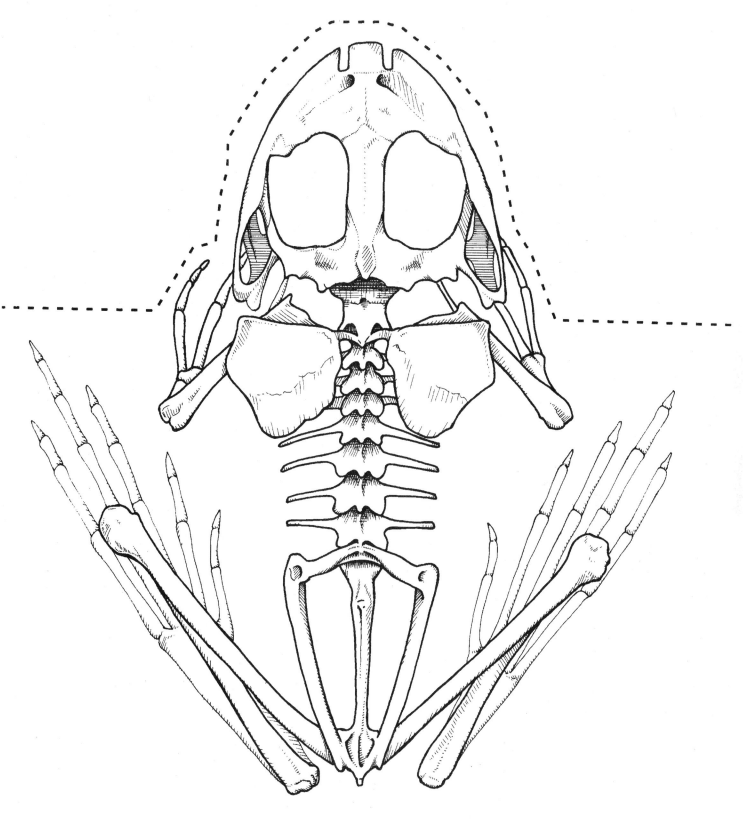

Simple Science Report

BAT

Provide books and other materials about bats for students reporting on this animal. (You may need to read these to younger students.) Discuss the information they have learned, then assign a writing task.

First Look at Bats by Millicent E. Selsam; Walker, 1991
Shadows of the Night: The Hidden World of the Little Brown Bat
by Barbara Bash; Sierra Club Books, 1993

Discussion Starters

How would you describe a bat?

How do bats find their way around in the dark?

What kinds of foods do bats eat?

What makes a bat a mammal?

In what ways are bats like birds?

How are bats different than birds?

Skeleton Discussion Starter

Look at the bones in the bat's wing. Can you find the bones that look like a thumband fingers? Do these bones remind you of any part of your body?

Writing Ideas

1. A Report about Bats
   a. Tell what a bat looks like.
   b. Tell how bats move.
   c. Tell what bats eat.
   d. Tell how a bat finds its food.

2. Compare a bat with a bird.

3. Do research on one special kind of bat. Write a report about it.

4. Write a story about a bat.

The Bat Who Stayed Awake All Day
If I Were a Bat
Bats in the Attic

Bats

There are almost 1000 kinds of bats spread over the earth. Some are as small as a jellybean and some are as big as a small dog. They come in many colors and patterns. These help the bats blend in with their surroundings.

Bats are mammals. They have furry bodies. Mother bats have live babies which are fed milk from the mother's body. A bat is the only mammal that can really fly.

Bats' wings are made of muscle, bones, and skin. Strong chest muscles help flap the wings. Bats use their tails for balance and making turns. They use curved claws on their feet to hang upside down. They don't fall even when they are asleep.

Insect-eating bats use their voice and hearing to find food. This is called echolocation. They have big ears to help them hear better. They catch in-sects as they fly through the air. Insect-eating bats eat millions of insects every night that might destroy our crops.

Fruit-eating bats use their eyes and sense of smell to find food. They eat fruit, flowers, fruit juice, or nectar. They have smaller ears than insect-eaters. Some have noses with strange flaps to help them catch smells better. They spread pollen from plant to plant as they eat. They also carry seeds from one place to another. This helps new plants to grow.

Bats eat other things too. Some bats eat frogs, rodents, fish, and other small animals. Vampire bats eat blood. They bite animals, but they don't usually bite humans. They lap up the blood like a kitten laps up milk.

Bats live in groups called colonies. Many colonies live in dark caves. Others roost in hollow logs, holes in trees, in tunnels made by other animals, or in people's barns and attics. Many kinds of fruit-eating bats live in trees. One bat even makes a leaf "tent" to use as a home. Some colonies are small. Others have over one million bats.

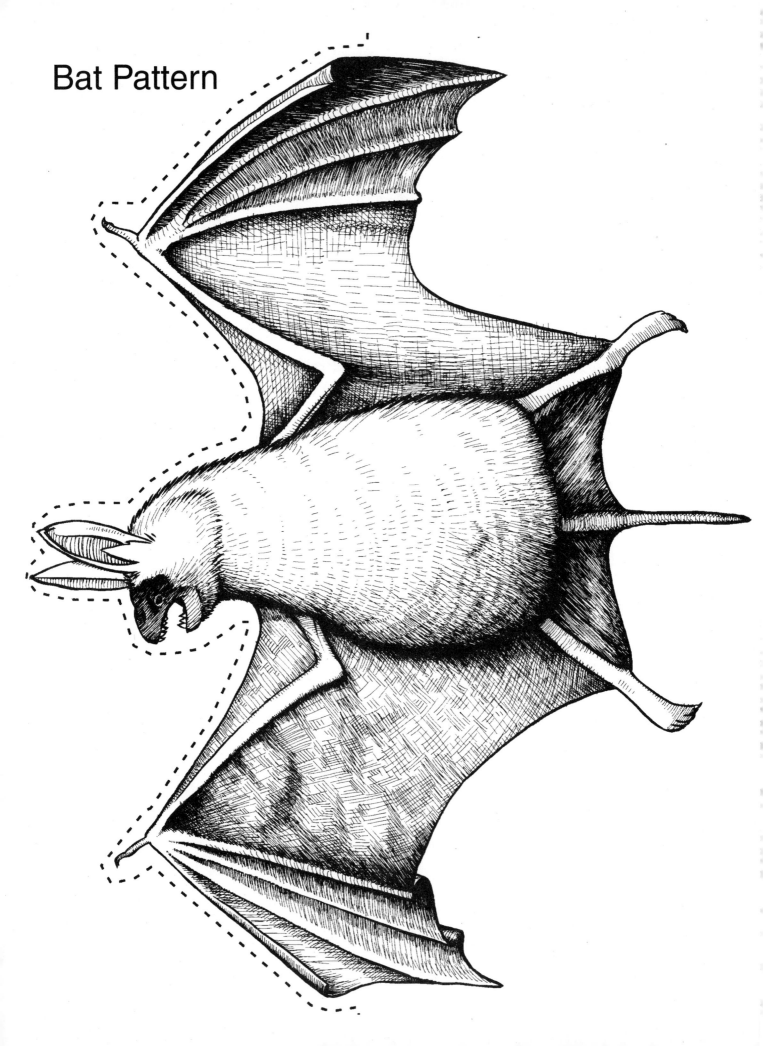

Bat Pattern

Bat Skeleton

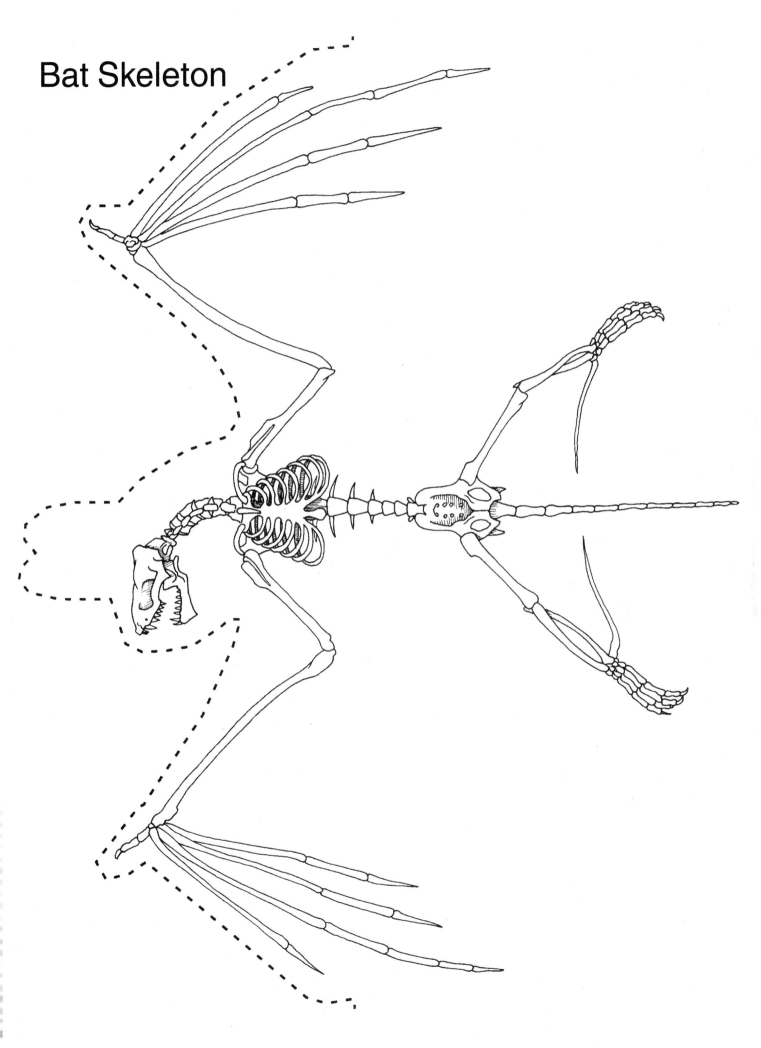

Simple Science Report
KILLER WHALE
(Orca)

Provide books and other materials about killer whales for students reporting on this animal. (You may need to read these to younger students.) Discuss the information they have learned, then assign a writing task.

Killer Whales by Dorothy Hinshaw Patent; Holiday House Inc., 1993
Killer Whales by S. Palmer; Rourke Corp. 1988

Discussion Starters

What kind of animal is a killer whale?

How can you tell?

How big is a killer whale?

Where does a killer whale live?

How does a killer whale get its food?

Why is a killer whale dark on top and light on the bottom?

Skeleton Discussion Starter

Look at the bones in the killer whale's flippers.
Do they remind you of anything?
Are there bones in the killer whale's tail flukes?
Can you tell what an orca eats by looking at its mouth?

Writing Ideas

1. A Report about Killer Whales
   a. Tell what a killer whale looks like.
   b. Tell how a killer whale moves.
   c. Tell what killer whales eat.
   d. Tell how killer whales catch their food.

2. Describe the environment in which a killer whale lives.

3. Compare a killer whale and a land hunter such as a wolf.

4. Write a story about a killer whale.

The Lost Killer Whale
How the Killer Whale Got its Name
If I Were an Orca

Killer Whale
(Orca)

Although whales live in the ocean, they are not fish. They are mammals like dogs and horses. They have special adaptations to help them live underwater.

Like all whales, killer whales have a blowhole on top of their head for breathing. This is where the old air comes out of a whale and new air comes in when it comes to the surface. The blowhole closes when the whale is underwater.

They have smooth, rubbery skin. Killer whales have black and white designs on their bodies. Whales have a layer of fat called blubber under their skin. This keeps them warm.

A whale's tail has two parts called flukes. Strong muscles pull the flukes up and down as the whale swims. Whales have flippers on their sides which help them swim. The flippers help them steer also. A fin on the whale's back helps keep the whale's body stable as it swims.

Killer whales are not large like whales such as the blue whale or the humpback whale. They are around 20 - 30 feet (6 - 9 meters) long.

Some whales have teeth and others have baleen (thick plates of material similar to fingernails). The orca or killer whale is a whale with teeth. Killer whales eat fish, seals, penguins, squid, and sea turtles. Killer whales often hunt together in a pack. This way they can hunt larger prey such as seals.

Killer whales live in groups called pods. They swim together and hunt together. Killer whales stay in the pod in which they were born even when they are grown.

Whale babies are born alive in the water. The mother helps her baby get to the surface for its first breath of air. She feeds the baby very rich milk. This helps the baby grow fast.

Killer Whale Pattern

Killer Whale Skeleton

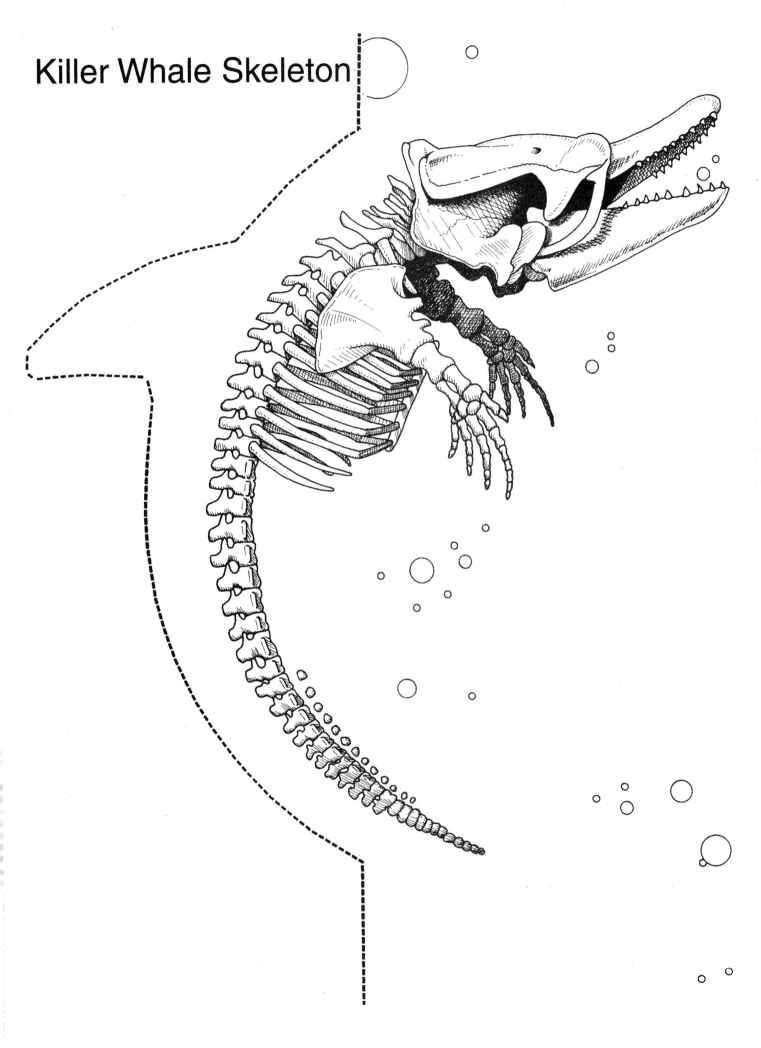

Simple Science Report

TORTOISE

Provide books and other materials about tortoises for students reporting on this animal. (You may need to read these to younger students.) Discuss the information they have learned, then assign a writing task.

Turtles and Tortoises by Vassili Papastavrou; Watts, 1992
The Galapagos Tortoise by Susan Schafer; Macmillan Childrens Group, 1992
Turtle and Tortoise by Vincent Serventy; Raintree Steck-Vaughn,1985

Discussion Starters

Where does the tortoise live?

What does a tortoise eat?

How does the shell protect the tortoise?

Is there a difference between a turtle and a tortoise?

Skeleton Discussion Starter

Look at the bones in the neck of the tortoise.
Can you describe how this helps protect the tortoise?

Writing Ideas

1. A Report about a Tortoise
   a. Tell what a tortoise looks like.
   b. Tell how a tortoise moves.
   c. Tell what a tortoise eats.
   d. Tell how a tortoise catches its food.

2. Describe how a tortoise and a turtle are alike and how they are different.

3. A tortoise has a strong shell for protection. What kind of a protective "shell" could a person wear?

4. Write a story about a tortoise.

In a Tortoise Nest
The Tortoise and the Hare - My Own Version
If I Were a Tortoise

Tortoise

A tortoise is a turtle that lives on land. Tortoises are reptiles like snakes and alligators. Tortoises have existed almost unchanged for millions of years.

A tortoise has a hard, bony shell and strong legs. Once a tortoise is grown, this heavy shell provides both shelter and protection against most enemies except for man. The tortoise can pull its long neck into the shell for safety. It has powerful legs, but these are needed to carry around the heavy shell rather than to make the tortoise move fast.

Some types of tortoises have sharp claws for digging. The desert tortoise of the American Southwest and the gopher tortoise of Florida dig burrows to escape the heat.

The Galapagos tortoise is very large. Some adult males weigh as much as 400 pounds (226 kg). But the largest tortoise of all is the Aldabran giant which weighs almost 600 pounds (272 kg).

Unless it is killed by a predator or in an accident, some kinds of tortoises can live as long as 100 years.

Tortoise Pattern

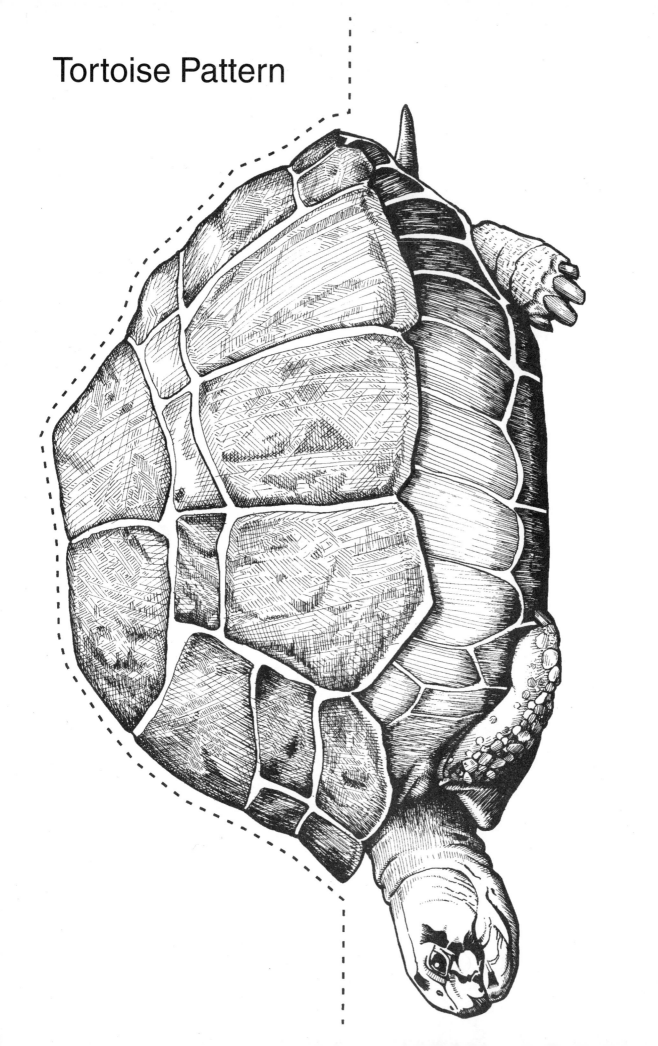

Tortoise Skeleton

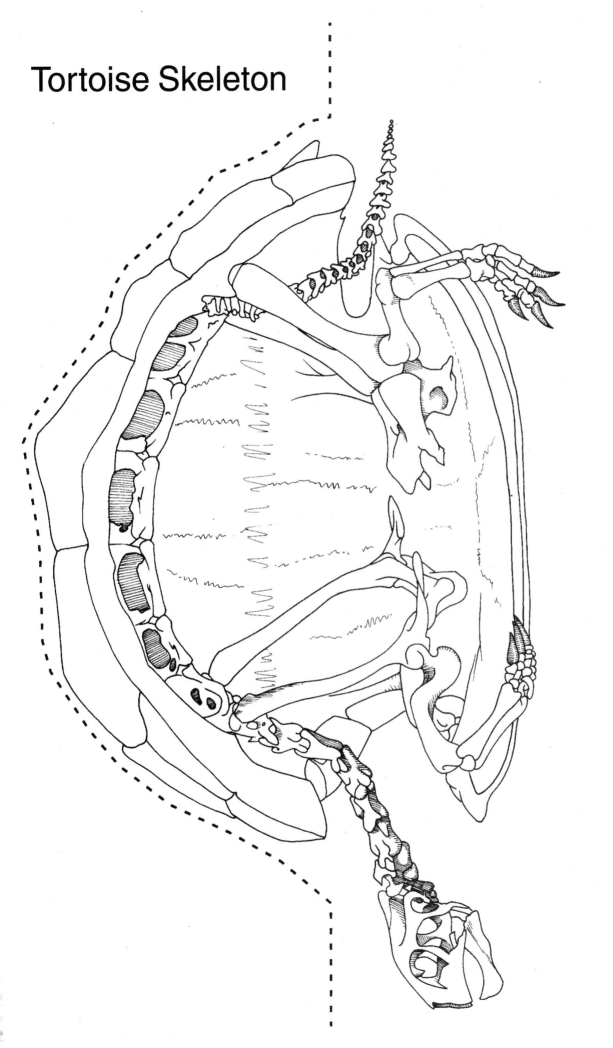

Simple Science Report

CROW

Provide books and other materials about crows for students reporting on this bird. (You may need to read these to younger students.) Discuss the information they have learned, then assign a writing task.

Our Yard is full of Birds by Anne Rockwell; Macmillan, 1992
What is a Bird? by Ron Hirschi; Walker and Co., 1987
A First Look at Birds by Millicent Selsam and Joyce Hunt; Walker, 1973

Discussion Starters:

What makes a crow a bird?

Why can a bird fly?

What do crows eat?

Why does a crow build a nest?

How does it care for its young?

Skeleton Discussion Starter:

Look at the crow's skull.
Can you find these parts?
> eye socket
> beak
> nostril holes

Writing Ideas:

1. A Report about Crows
   a. Tell what a crow looks like.
   b. Tell how a crow moves.
   c. Tell what a crow eats.
   d. Tell about the life cycle of a crow.

2. Write an explanation of why a farmer might not like crows.

3. Explain how a crow and a blue jay are alike and how they are different.

4. Write a story about a crow.

My Talking Crow
The Magpie Who Was a Thief
If I Were a Crow

Crow

Crows are large, noisy birds. They live in the open countryside. The common crow is a pest to farmers. Although crows help by eating insects, they also eat seeds and grains and can damage a farmer's crops. They are too smart to be fooled by a scarecrow for very long.

Crows eat other things also. They eat fruit, small mammals, and dead animals. They will also eat birds' eggs and baby birds still in the nest.

Crows have a loud call of their own, but some are good mimics and can imitate the sound of other birds, animals, and even human speech.

Some types are attracted to shiny objects and will fly off with them.

There are 116 kinds of crows living around the world. The raven is the largest crow. It has a wingspan of 6 feet (2 meters). Jackdaws, living in Europe, build nests in tree holes and on chimney tops.

Although we think of black when we think of crows, the colorful jay is a part of the crow family. Jays live in woodlands and parks.

 Simple Science Reports

Crow Pattern

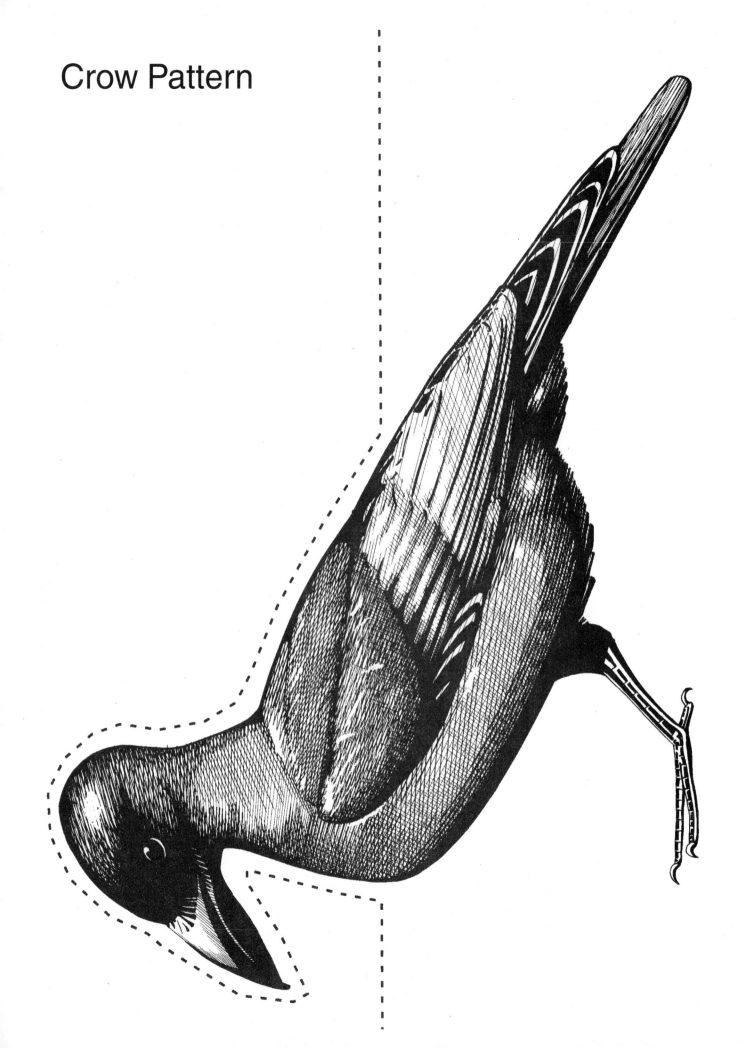

Crow Skeleton

Simple Science Report
CROCODILE

Provide books and other materials about crocodiles for students reporting on this animal. (You may need to read these to younger students.) Discuss the information they have learned, then assign a writing task.

Crocodiles and Alligators by Norman S. Barrett; Watts, 1991
I Can Read About Alligators and Crocodiles by David Knight; Troll, 1979

Discussion Starters
Can you describe the place a crocodile lives?
Why are a crocodile's eyes on top of its head?
Where does a crocodile mother lay her eggs?
How does a crocodile capture its food?
What makes a crocodile a reptile?

Skeleton Discussion Starter
Can you tell what a crocodile probably eats by looking at its skeleton? How did you decide?

Writing Ideas
1. A Report about Crocodiles
   a. Tell what a crocodile looks like.
   b. Tell how a crocodile moves.
   c. Tell what a crocodile eats.
   d. Tell how a crocodile gets its food.

2. Describe how a crocodile is adapted to life in the water.

3. Compare a crocodile and an alligator.

4. Write a story about crocodiles.

A Strange Egg in the Crocodile's Nest
Escape from a Crocodile
If I Were a Crocodile

Crocodile

Crocodiles are reptiles like alligators, snakes, and turtles. They have thick, leathery, scaly skin. Crocodiles live in the water.

A crocodile's eyes and nostrils are set high on their heads. It can see what is going on and can breathe without raising its head out of the water. Underwater, it keeps its nostrils and ears closed. It can hold its breath for more than an hour.

A crocodile swims quickly by moving its long powerful tail back and forth sideways in the water. It can swim slowly through the water using just its feet. When danger threatens, it sinks down deep in the water.

A crocodile comes ashore to lay on the riverbanks in the hot sun. It comes ashore to catch food if an animal is foolish enough to be caught close to the riverbank. It also comes ashore to lay eggs.

A crocodile has about 100 teeth. The teeth are good for holding food, but not for chewing it. A crocodile holds food in its teeth and thrashes it about to tear it apart. Food is swallowed in large hunks. It eats fish, birds, snakes, lizards, frogs, turtles, rats, deer, zebra, and cattle. A crocodile will eat both living and dead animals.

A crocodile's powerful jaws are its best weapon. Once the jaws are closed tight, no animal can escape its grip. It also has good sight and hearing. Crocodiles keep in touch with each other using different sounds.

Crocodiles lay hard-shelled eggs. The eggs are often just buried in the sand. The babies peep loudly when they hatch so the mother can help them out of the nest. Newborn crocodiles cannot look after themselves very well. The mother usually tries to protect them for the first few months, sometimes carrying them from the nest to the water in her mouth. Many will still by eaten by other animals.

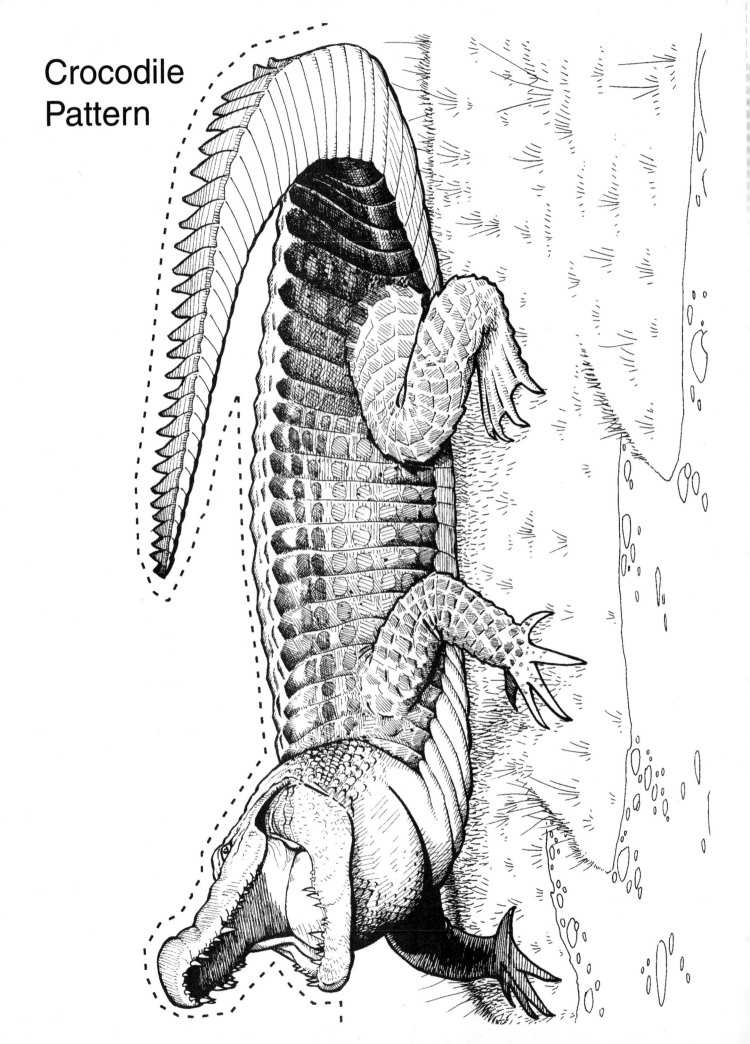

Crocodile
Pattern

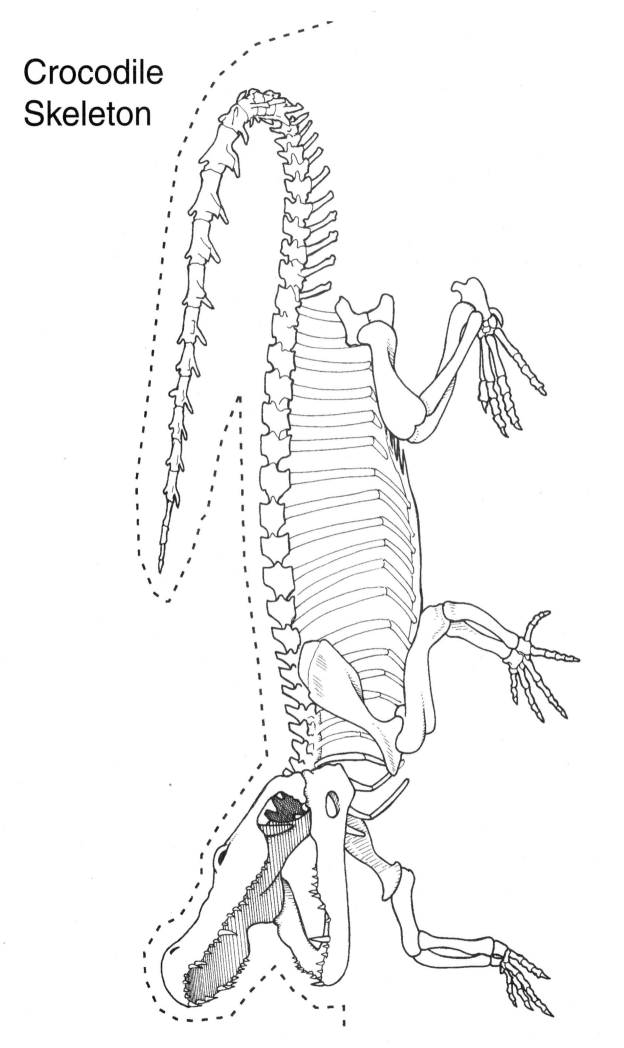

Crocodile
Skeleton

Simple Science Report
GRAY SQUIRREL

Provide books and other materials about gray squirrels for students reporting on this animal. (You may need to read these to younger students.) Discuss the information they have learned, then assign a writing task.

Squirrels by Emilie Lepthien; Childrens Press, 1993
The Squirrel by Margaret Lane; Dial, 1981
The World of Squirrels by Jennifer Coldrey; Gareth Stevens, 1986

Discussion Starters

How does a gray squirrel prepare for winter?

What kind of food does the gray squirrel eat?

Why do you think the gray squirrel makes its home in a tree?

Does a squirrel lay eggs or have live babies?

How does its gray fur help protect the squirrel?

Skeleton Discussion Starter

Why does a gray squirrel's tail look so big when it has such tiny bones in the skeleton?

Writing Ideas

1. A Report about the Gray Squirrel
   a. Tell what a gray squirrel looks like.
   b. Tell how a gray squirrel moves.
   c. Tell what a gray squirrel eats and how it gets its food.
   d. Describe where a gray squirrel lives.

2. Describe the ways in which a gray squirrel uses its tail.

3. Explain how tree squirrels and ground squirrels are alike and how they are different.

4. Write a story about a gray squirrel.

Gray Squirrel Gets Ready for Winter
The Fabulous Squirrel Acrobat
If I Were a Gray Squirrel

Squirrels

Most squirrels are similar to rats and mice in shape, but they have bushy tails. There are tree squirrels such as red, gray, and flying squirrels that live in woodland areas, often high up in trees. There are also ground squirrels which have shorter tails and never climb trees.

Gray squirrels live where there are trees. They are well adapted for living in trees. Squirrels use their sharp claws for clinging to the bark of trees. They use their fluffy tail to help keep their balance as they move along tree branches. Squirrels are able to leap through the trees easily.

Squirrels build bulky, ball-shaped nests in the forks of tree branches. Sometimes they build their nests in hollow tree trunks. Squirrels rest and sleep in these nests of twigs and leaves. They also raise their young in these nests.

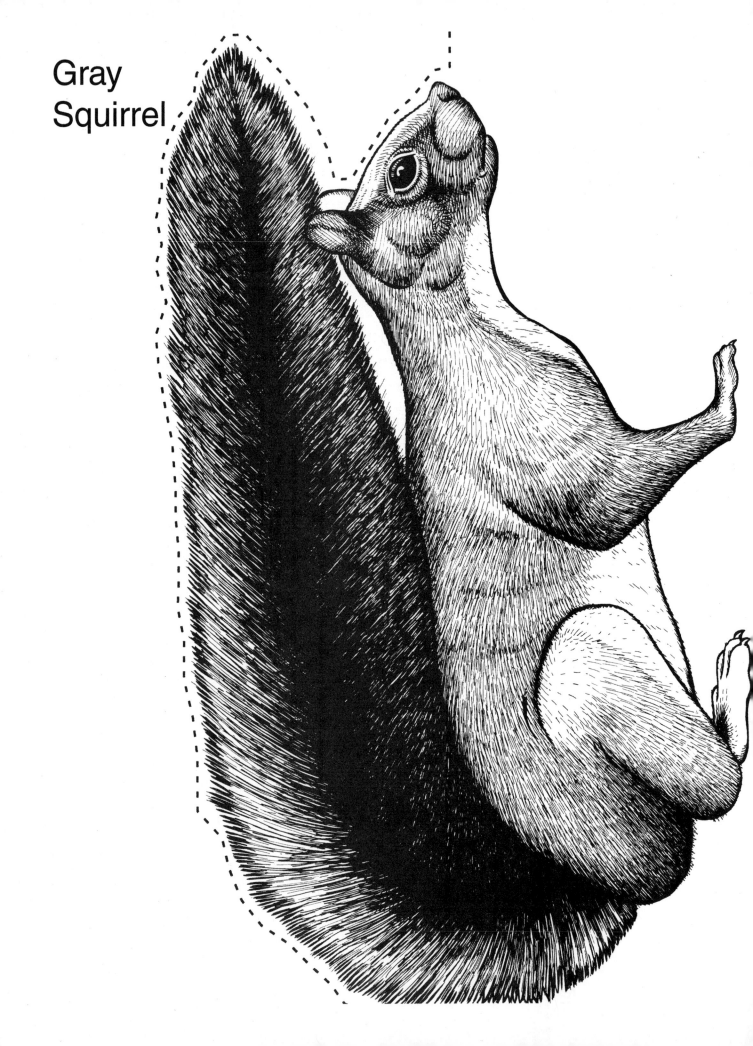

Gray
Squirrel

Gray
Squirrel
Skeleton

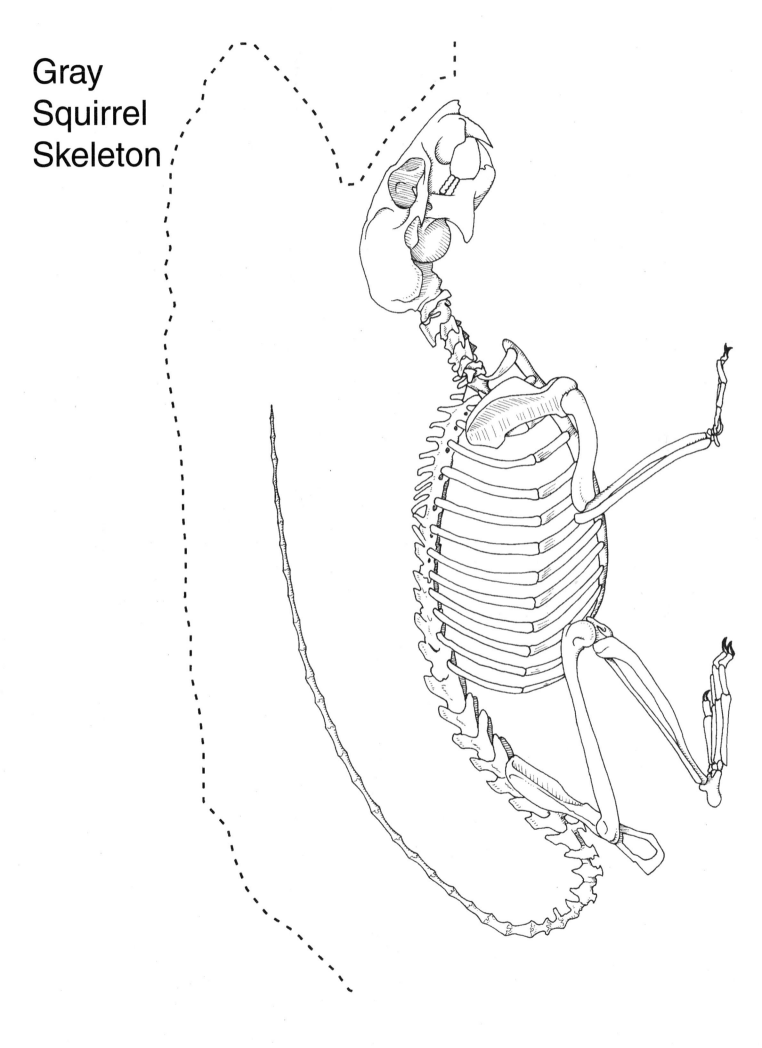

Simple Science Report

LION

Provide books and other materials about lions for students reporting on this animal. (You may need to read these to younger students.) Discuss the information they have learned, then assign a writing task.

Big Cats by Seymour Simon; Harper, 1991
The Lion Family by Angelika Hofer and Gunter Ziesler; Picture Book, 1988
Lions by Wildlife Staff; Wildlife Education, 1992

Discussion Starters

Does a lion build some sort of a house?

Where does a lion live?

What does it eat?

How does it capture its food?

How are lions like pet cats?

How are they different than pet cats?

Skeleton Discussion Starter

Can you tell how the lion gets its food by looking at its skeleton?

Writing Ideas

1. A Report about Lions
   a. Tell what a lion looks like.
   b. Tell what a lion eats.
   c. Tell how a lion gets food.
   d. Describe a lion pride.

2. Tell how a lion and a pet cat are alike and how they are different.

3. Describe how a lion hunts for food.

4. Write a story about a lion.

The Lion Who Was Afraid
Life in a Lion Pride
If I Were a Lion

Lion

Lions are large members of the cat family. They live on the plains and in the woodlands of Africa. Lions are excellent hunters. They are also excellent "resters." They spend about 19 hours a day resting and 5 hours awake and active.

Lions are predators with strong, razor-sharp teeth and claws. They have strong bodies and excellent senses. They can see small objects at a distance and have a very good sense of smell and hearing. Their ears move so they can hear sounds coming from any direction. Their coloring helps them hide among trees and bushes to lay in ambush for unwary prey.

Lions are the only big cats that live in groups. These groups are called prides. There can be as many as 30 lions in a pride. The pride will consist of adult females with their cubs and one or more males. Both male and female lions help protect the pride's territory from outside lions. Lions have a much better chance of surviving if they belong to a pride.

Lions roam over a large area when they are hunting prey. They hunt in groups. Usually it is the lionesses who do the hunting. After a successful kill, the males join the females and claim their share. They usually eat grass-eating animals such as wildebeests, gazelle, zebra, and buffalo.

Baby lions are born alive. There are usually two to four cubs in a litter. Lion cubs are very weak and clumsy when they are born. Their eyes are closed. Their mother must feed them milk and protect them from danger. After a few weeks, the cubs follow mother when she hunts, but they will not be able to hunt on their own until they are about 18 months old. The cubs spend a lot of time playing. This playtime is very important. It is how the cubs learn how grown-up lions are supposed to behave. It is how they learn hunting skills.

 Simple Science Reports

Lion Pattern

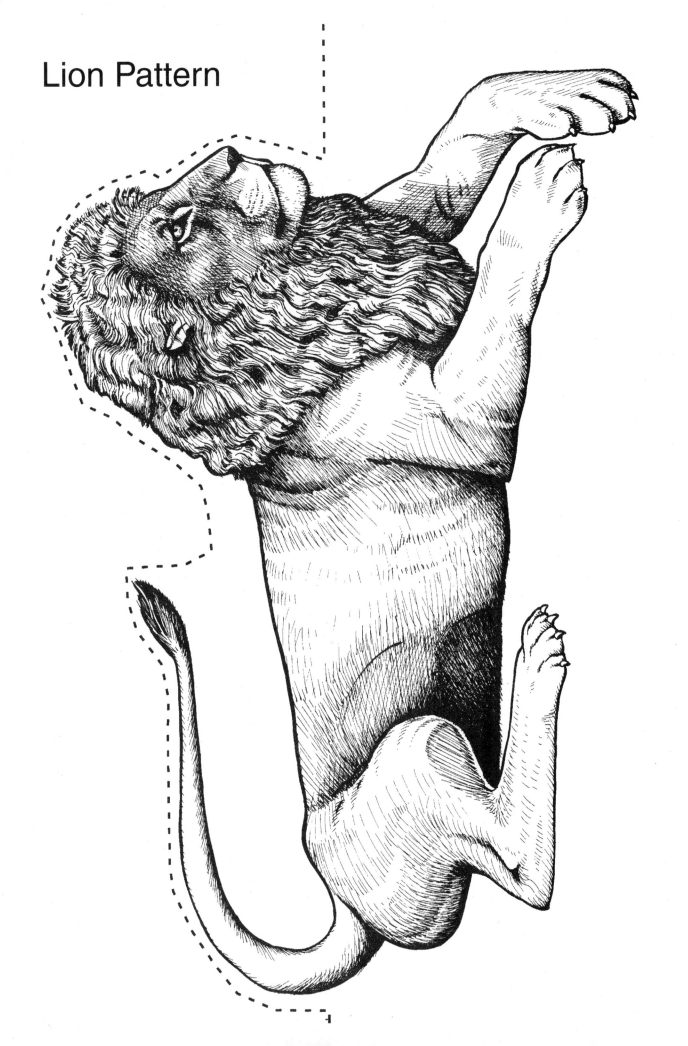

Lion Skeleton

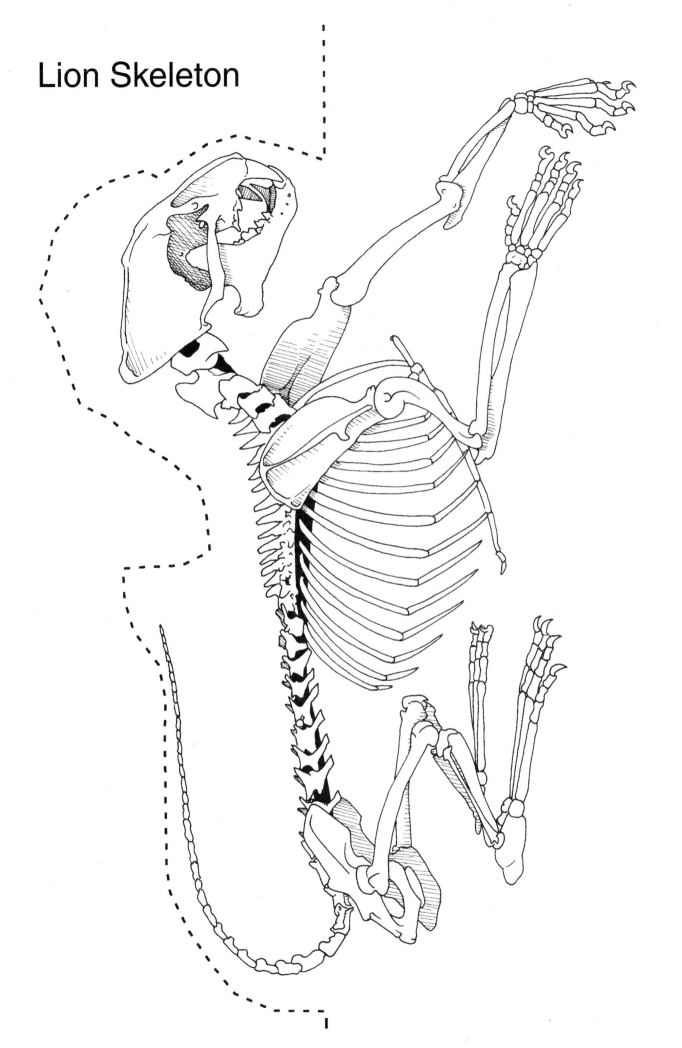

Simple Science Report

GORILLA

Provide books and other materials about gorillas for students reporting on this animal. (You may need to read these to younger students.) Discuss the information they have learned, then assign a writing task.

Gorilla by Robert McClung; William Morrow, 1984
Gorilla by Ian Redmond; Bookwright Press, 1991
Jane Goodall's Animal World: Gorillas by Jane Goodall; Macmillan
Childrens Group, 1990

Discussion Starters

Where do gorillas live?
What is a gorilla's habitat like?
What do gorillas eat?
What is special about a gorilla's hand?
How does a gorilla protect itself?

Skeleton Discussion Starter

Look at the gorilla's long arm bones. Why do you think they are important for the gorilla?

Writing Ideas

1. A Report about Gorillas
    a. Tell what a gorilla looks like.
    b. Tell what gorillas eat.
    c. Tell how a gorilla moves.
    d. Describe a gorilla's habitat.

2. Mountain gorillas are endangered animals. Write at least three reasons why you think they should be protected.

3. Do you think gorillas should be kept in zoos? Explain your opinion.

4. Write a story about a gorilla.

Help! A Gorilla is Loose in the City
The Mischievous Little Gorilla
If I Were a Gorilla

Gorillas

Gorillas live in the dense African jungles. Gorillas are the largest, most powerful of the apes. An adult male gorilla can weigh as much as 525 pounds (240 kilograms). Gorillas are the most intelligent animals. They are usually quiet and gentle animals.

Gorillas live in small family groups. Each group is made up of one adult male, a number of females and their young. These groups are called troops.

Most of the time, gorillas lead a peaceful life. They spend much of the day feeding since they need a lot of food to survive. They eat mostly leaves and fruit. In between eating, they rest. At night, gorillas make platform nests of twigs and branches either on the ground or in low trees.

The gorilla is the only ape that lives on the ground. Gorillas spend more time on the ground than up in the trees. Young gorillas may play in the trees.

Gorillas walk on flat feet and the knuckles of their hands.

The habitat of the gorilla is being destroyed. Many of the trees the gorilla lives in are being cut down so that coffee and other foods can be grown and sold. If man continues to cut down the trees, the gorilla will have no place to live or food to eat.

Gorilla
Pattern

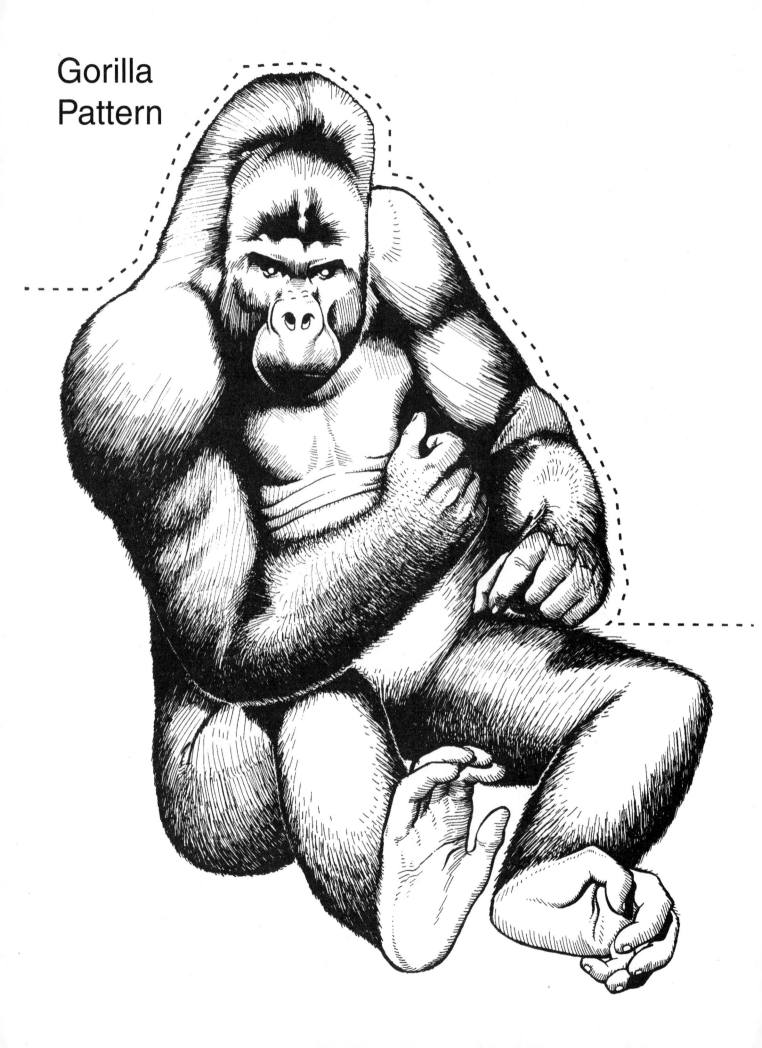

Gorilla
Skeleton

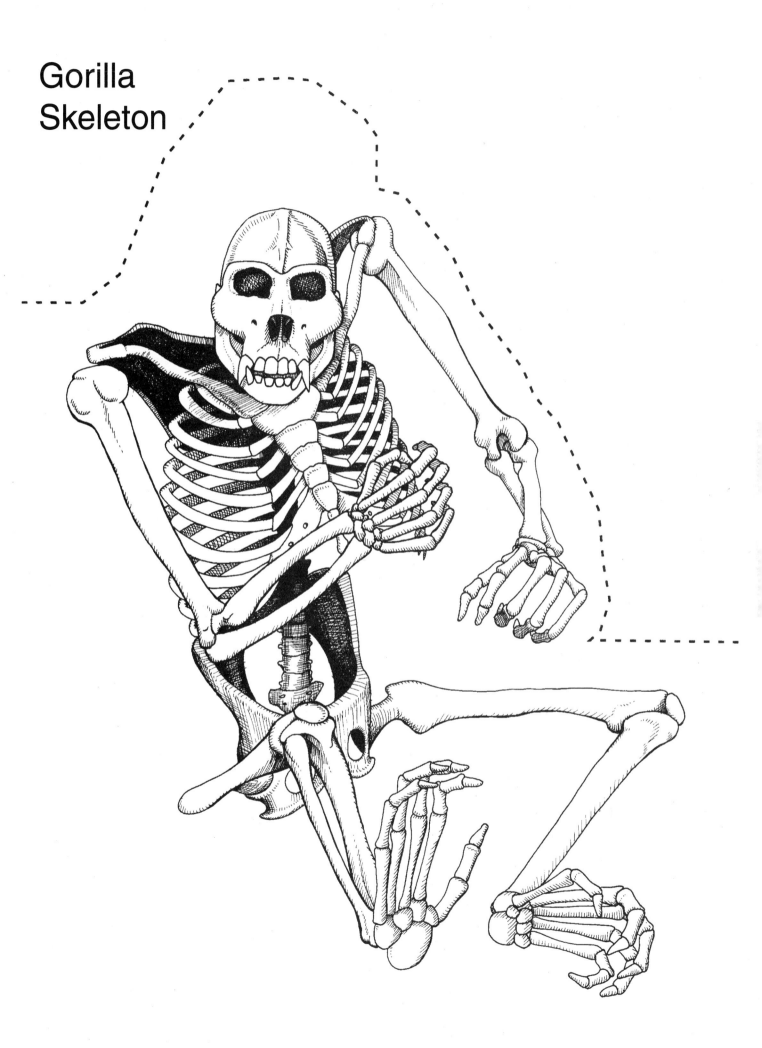

Simple Science Report

KOALA

Provide books and other materials about koalas for students reporting on this animal. (You may need to read these to younger students.) Discuss the information they have learned, then assign a writing task.

Koalas by Sandra Lee; Child's World, 1993
Koala by Vincent Serventy; Steck-Vaughn, 1992

Discussion Starters

What kind of an animal is a koala?

Why does the baby have to spend such a long time in the mother's pouch?

How does a koala take care of her baby?

Why does the koala spend its life in eucalyptus trees?

In what country do koalas live?

Skeleton Discussion Starter

What can you tell about how they live by looking at a koala's feet?

Writing Idea

1. A Report about Koalas
   a. Tell what a koala looks like.
   b. Tell what a koala eats.
   c. Describe where a koala lives.
   d. Tell how a koala raises its baby.

2. A koala uses her pouch to carry her baby around. You don't have a pouch.
   Make a list of all the different things you use to carry your belongings from place to place.

3. Describe how your life would be different if you lived in a tree.

4. Write a story about a koala.

Raising a Baby Koala
Lost in a Eucalyptus Forest
If I Were a Koala

Koala

Koalas are a very special type of mammal that live in Australia. They have thick fur to keep them warm and dry. Their babies are born live like other mammals and the babies are fed milk from the mother's body. But koalas have a special pouch on their underside where they carry their babies.

When a koala baby is born it is only about the size of a lima bean. It is blind and has no hair. The baby must crawl up into its mother's pouch. When it is safely in the pouch, the baby attaches itself to one of its mother's two teats. The teat swells inside the baby's mouth and holds the tiny koala safely in place. For many months the baby stays inside the pouch as it grows into a furry koala. Even after the baby koala is big enough to come out it will hop back into the pouch when it is frightened or when it wants to sleep or drink milk. After it is out of the pouch, the baby koala rides on its mother's back until it is big enough to look after itself.

A koala has a large nose and an excellent sense of smell which it uses to sniff each leaf before eating it. If the leaf does not smell right, the koala will try a different one. The favorite foods of koalas are the leaves of eucalyptus (gum) trees. They eat the tender shoots that grow on the tips of the branches. A koala has two sharp teeth in front of its mouth for tearing leaves or stripping bark. It has flat teeth in back for chewing the leaves. A koala usually only goes on the ground to move to a new tree.

Although "koala" means "drinks no water" in the language of the Australian aborigines, koalas do sometimes drink. The eucalyptus leaves provide most of the water they need.

Koalas are nocturnal animals. This means that they are more active at night than during the day. A koala doesn't have a home or a nest. It just wedges its body into the fork of a tree, wraps its arm or leg around a branch and closes its eyes.

 Simple Science Reports

Koala Pattern

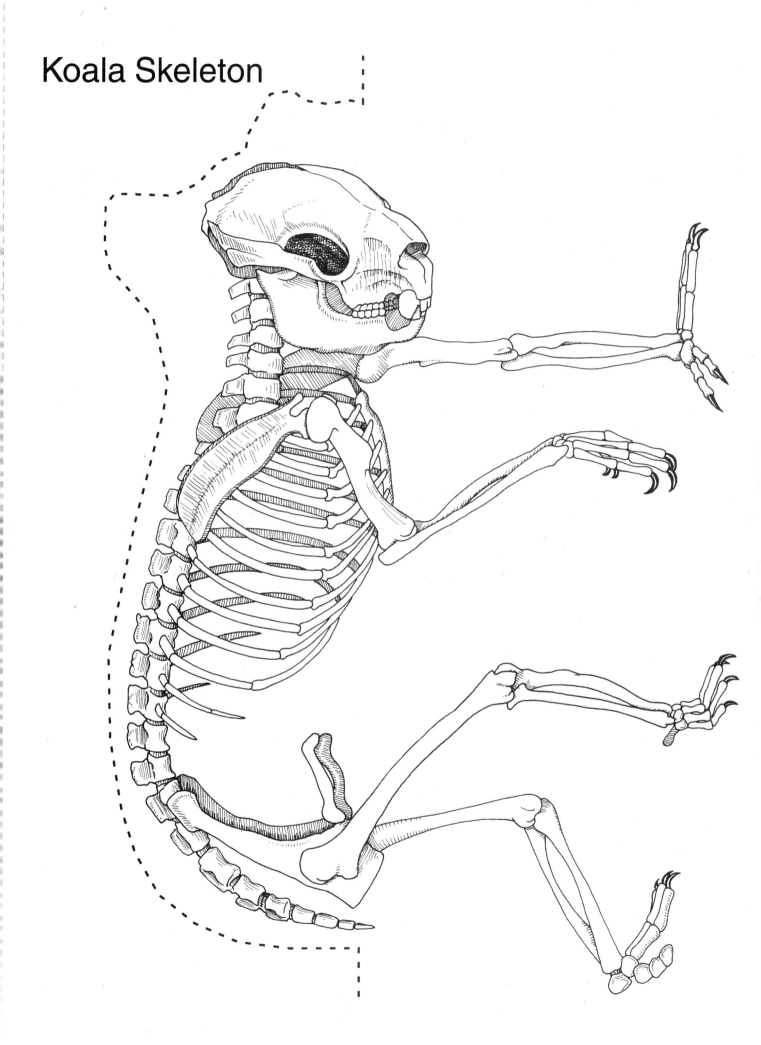

Koala Skeleton

Simple Science Reports

Part II
ANIMAL HOMES

Contents

Bibliography

Who Lives Here? by Dawn Brunke; North Word, 1993 (4 volumes)
Animal Homes by Joyce Pope; Troll, 1993
Animals' Homes; Dorling Kindersley, 1993
Burrows by Shirley Greenway; Newington, 1991
Animals Build Amazing Homes by Hedda Nassbaum;
Random Books for Young Readers, 1979

Provide books and other materials about beavers and their homes for students reporting on beaver lodges. (You may need to read these to younger students.) Discuss the information they have learned, then assign a writing task.

> **Busy Beavers** by Donald Crump; National Geography, 1988
> **The Beaver** by Margaret Lane; Dial Books for Young Readers, 1993
> **Beavers** by Peter Murray; Child's World, 1992

Discussion Starters

Where does a beaver build its lodge?

What materials does it use?

What parts of its body does a beaver use in building the lodge?

How does a beaver store food for the winter?

Animal Home Discussion Starter

Look at the picture of the inside of a beaver lodge. Why do you think the beaver builds the living room above water and the tunnels under water?

Writing Ideas

1. A Report about a Beaver Lodge
   a. Tell about who lives in a beaver lodge.
   b. Tell how a beaver lodge is built.
   c. Tell why this is a good home for beavers.

2. Compare a beaver "builder" and a human "builder."

3. Pretend you are out in the woods with only an axe and a rope. You must build yourself a shelter. How would you do this?

4. Write a story about a beaver and its lodge.

> **A Leak in the Beaver Dam**
> **A Beaver in Our Backyard**
> **The Beaver King's Castle**

Beaver Lodge

Beavers are rodents like mice, rats, gophers, and squirrels. Beavers are great builders. They build wonderful homes called lodges. They build these homes on lakes and rivers. Before they build a lodge, beavers build a dam across the stream. This makes a pool of still water around the home they build. Families of beavers work together to build a lodge.

Beavers use their sharp, chisel-like teeth to gnaw at trees and cut them down. They float the logs and branches along the water to the place they plan to build the dam. It takes many logs to make a dam. The logs are held in place by a kind of "cement" made of mud, leaves, and sticks. Other branches are used to build the lodge.

The beaver's lodge looks like a big pile of tree branches and mud. The mound is above water level. Inside the mound is a large room where the beavers eat, sleep, and raise their babies. The entrances are always below water so the beaver can go in and out of the lodge in safety.

All autumn long beavers store tree shoots and bark near the lodge to eat during winter when food is scarce.

Simple Science Reports

Beaver Lodge

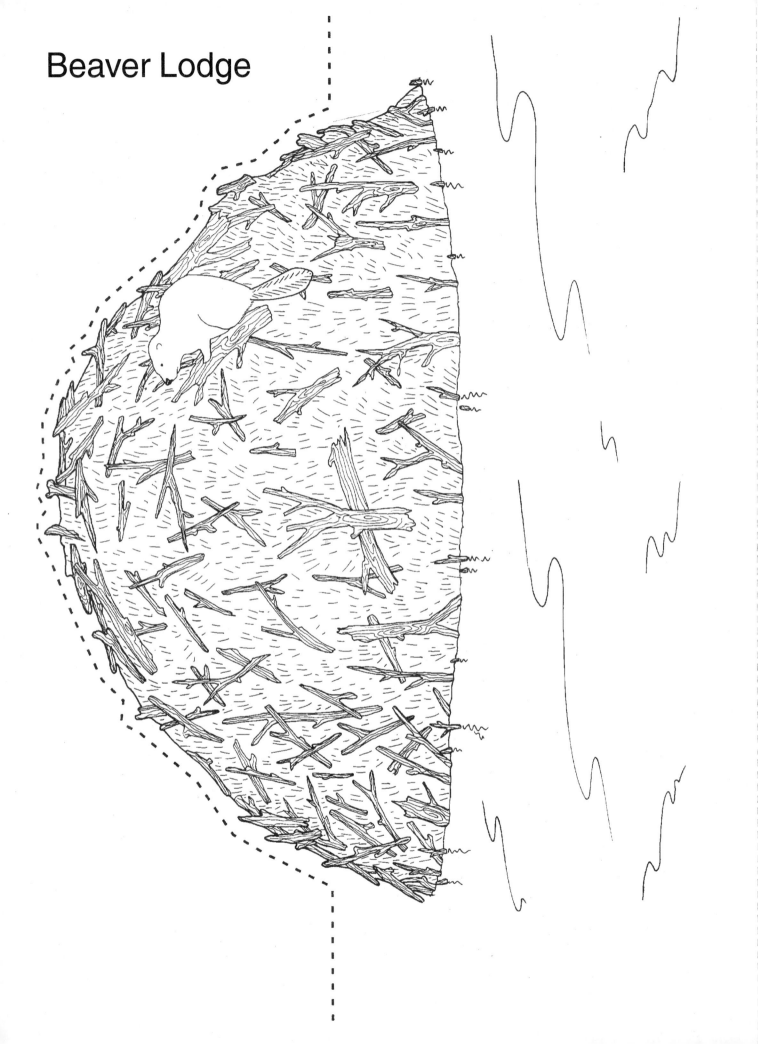

Inside the
Beaver Lodge

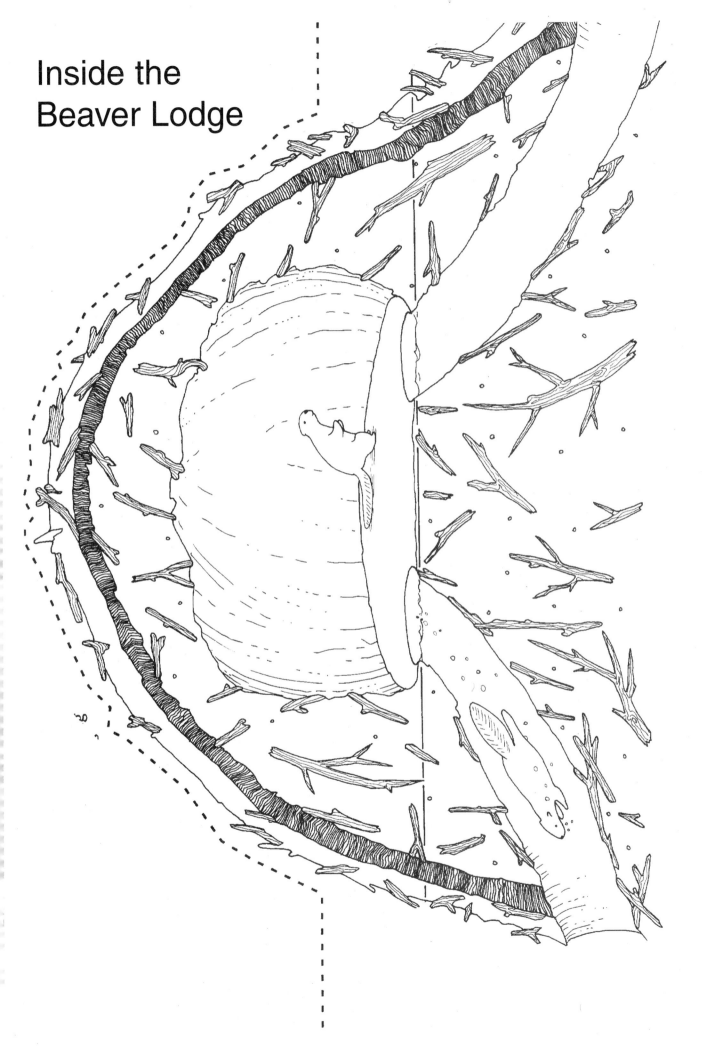

Simple Science Report
BIRD NEST

Provide books and other materials about birds and their nests for students reporting on bird nests. (You may need to read these to younger students.) Discuss the information they have learned, then assign a writing task.

A First Look at Birds' Nests by Millicent Selsam; Walker and Co., 1984
Making a Nest by Paul Bennett; Thompson Learning, 1994
Birds' Nest, by Barrie Watts; Silver Burdett Press, 1986
Bird Egg Feather Nest, by Maryjo Koch; Collins Publishers, 1994

Discussion Starters

What did the bird use to build the nest?

Where does the bird get the material for its nest?

Do all birds build nests?

Do all nest-building birds make the same type of nest?

Why do you think different kinds of birds have different kinds of nests?

Animal Home Discussion Starter

Look at the picture of the inside of this nest carefully. Do you think this is a safe home for the eggs and for baby birds? Why?

Writing Ideas

1. A Report about Birds' Nests
   a. Tell about who lives in a nest.
   b. Tell how a nest is built.
   c. Tell why this is a good home for a bird.

2. Not all birds build nests. Describe some of the dangers a bird's eggs and hatchlings face if they are not in a nest.

3. Describe the kind of nest you would build if you were a bird. What material would you use? What would the nest look like? What would your eggs look like?

4. Write a story about a bird and its nest.

Too Many Eggs in the Nest
Building a Nest on a Windy Day
The Brave Mother Bird

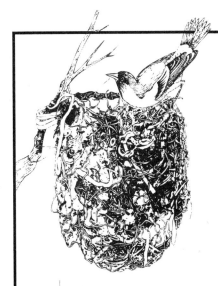

Bird Nests

Some birds build nests in trees. Some birds make simple nests on the ground. Some birds don't make any nest. The cuckoo lays her eggs in other birds' nests.

Nests come in all shapes and sizes. There are little cup-shaped nests, fancy woven nests, and nests made of huge piles of branches. Each type of bird builds its own kind of nest. A nest can tell you what kind of bird made it and can tell you about the bird's habitat.

Instinct tells a bird what type of nest to build. The nest is created from materials in the bird's habitat. A bird living by a pond will use reeds and grasses in its nest. A bird in the city will use twigs and grass, but may also use hair, string, and other items left around by people. Some birds even use mud for a cozy nest.

A bird makes hundreds of trips to get enough of the right kinds of material to build its nest. Each bit of material is carefully worked into the nest to make it the right size and shape.

Birds use both materials they find in nature and materials that are man-made. If you were to take a nest apart you might find dry grass, moss, feathers, seeds, twigs, sticks, and animal fur from nature. You might find bits of string, cloth, tin foil, paper, and plastic left about by people.

         Simple Science Reports

Bird Nest Pattern
Baltimore Oriole

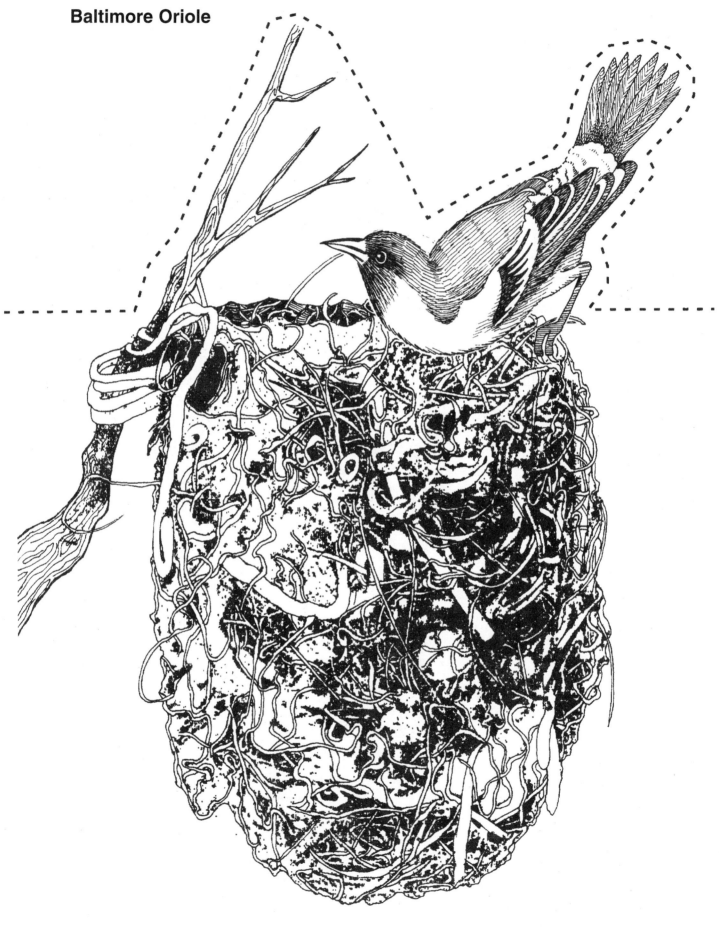

Inside the Bird Nest

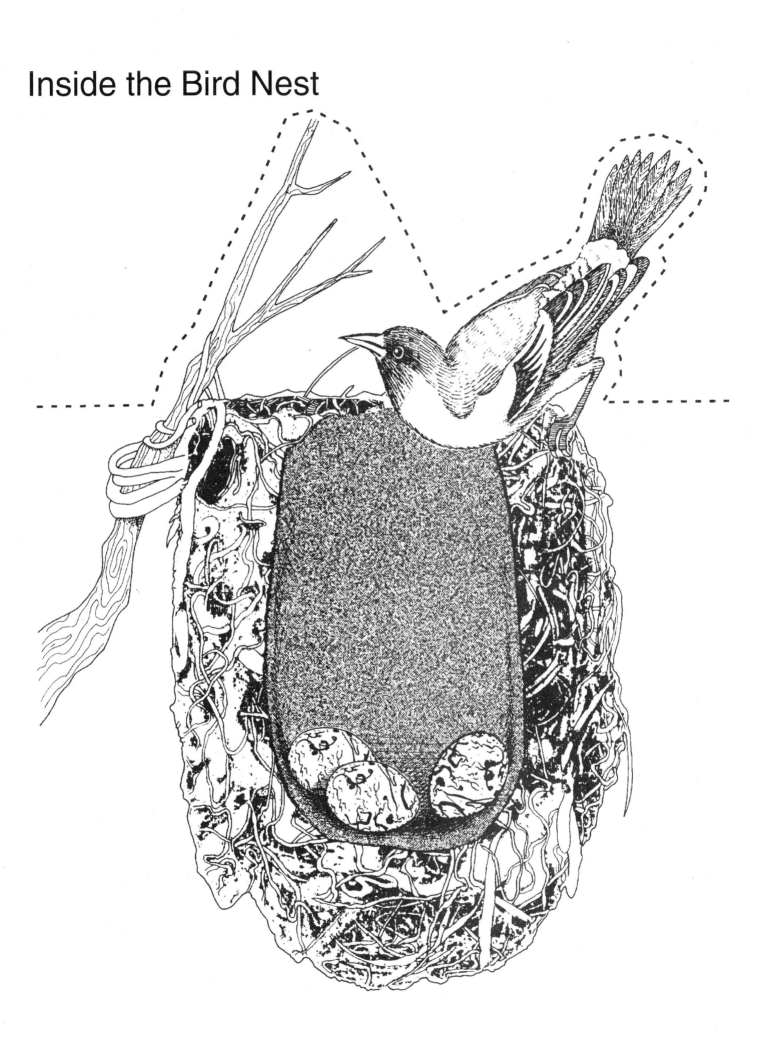

Simple Science Report

ANT HILL

Provide books and other materials about ants and their homes for students reporting on ant hills. (You may need to read these to younger students.) Discuss the information they have learned, then assign a writing task.

Ants by Cynthia Overbeck; Lerner, 1982
Ants by Edward Ross; Child's World, Inc., 1993
Ant Cities by Arthur Dorros; Harper Collins Childrens Books, 1993

Discussion Starters

Do all kinds of ants build the same kind of ant hill?

What kinds of jobs do different ants have?

What do ants eat and where do they get the food?

How do ants take care of their babies?

How do ants communicate with one another?

Animal Home Discussion Starter

Look at the picture of the inside of an ant hill.
Can you tell how the ant uses the different "rooms"?

Writing Ideas

1. A Report about an Ant Hill
   a. Tell about who lives in an ant hill.
   b. Tell how an ant hill is built.
   c. Tell why this is a good home for ants.

2. Make a list of all the kinds of animals you know that live in tunnels under the ground.

3. Describe how an ant hill is like your home and how it is different than your home.

4. Write a story about ants and an ant hill.

The Little Lost Ant
Protecting the Ant Hill
If I Lived in an Ant Hill

Ant Hill

Ants build nests in all kinds of places. Some build tunnels in the rotten wood of logs or telephone poles. Some nest in branches of living trees. The kinds of ants we see the most build their nests in the earth.

In these nests built under the earth, whole communities of ants are busily working away. The ants build homes with many rooms and tunnels where they live, store their food, and raise their young.

An ant hill in the ground begins with one small room that the queen makes before she lays her eggs. The workers ants dig tunnels leading from the queen's room to the surface. The worker then start building underground tunnels and many more rooms. They dig out the dirt and carry it, bit by bit, up to the surface. Some kinds of ants carry the dirt away from the opening and scatter it around. Other kinds of ants let the dirt pile up around the entrance to the nest.

The workers dig rooms to use as nurseries for the eggs, larvae, and pupae stages of the baby ants. They build rooms in which to store food. And they build rooms to use as resting places for the worker ants.

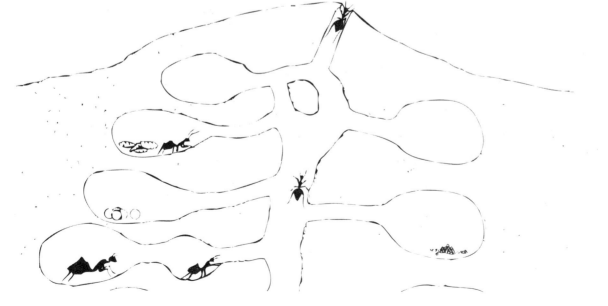

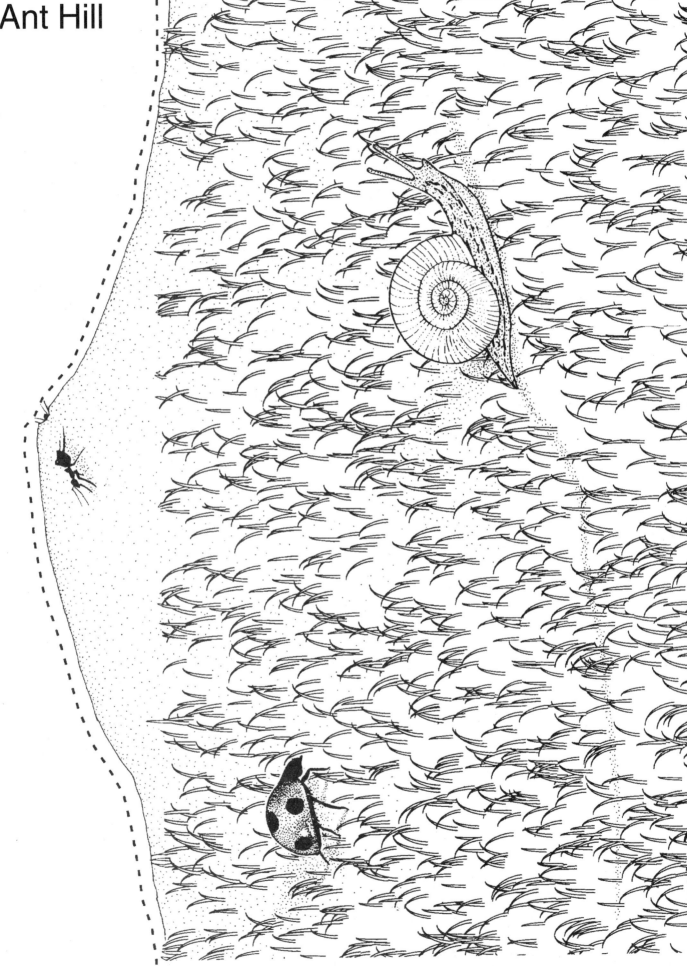

Ant Hill

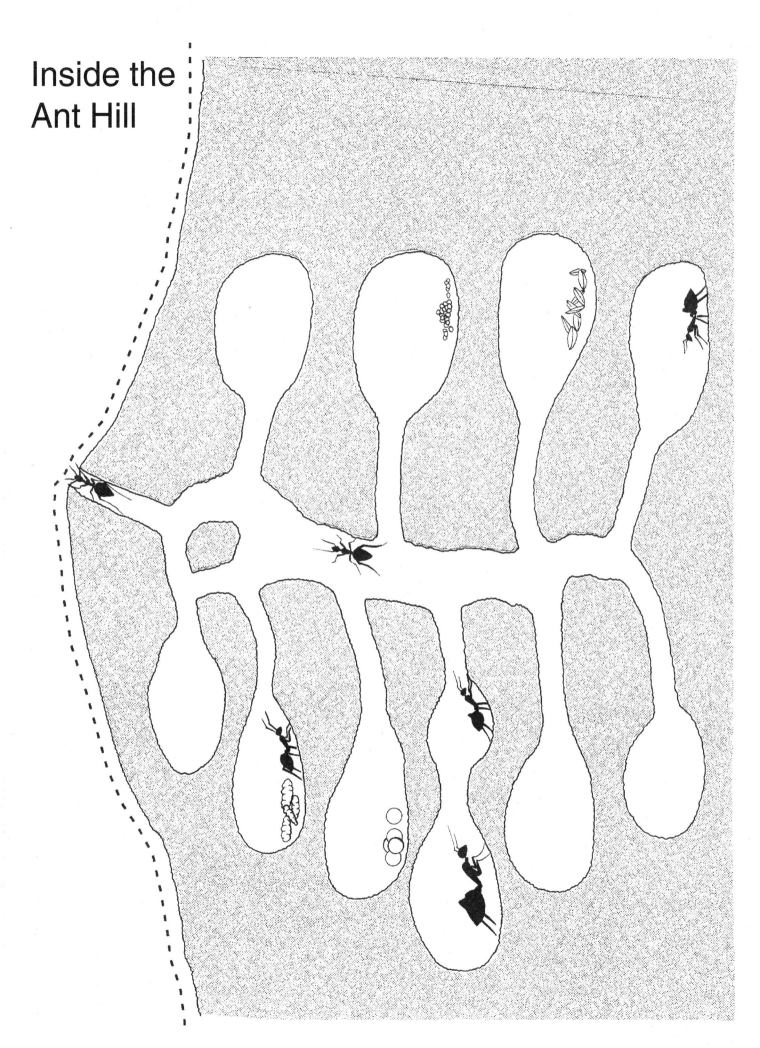

Inside the
Ant Hill

Simple Science Report
GRAY SQUIRREL NEST

Provide books and other materials about squirrels and their homes for students reporting on squirrel nests. (You may need to read these to younger students.) Discuss the information they have learned, then assign a writing task.

The Squirrel in the Trees by Jennifer Coldrey; Gareth Stevens, 1987
The World of Squirrels by Jennifer Coldrey; Gareth Stevens, 1987

Discussion Starters

What do gray squirrels use to build their nests?

Where do they build nests?

Why do they build nests in trees?

What does a squirrel keep in the nest?

Do all squirrels build nests?

How is a squirrel's nest different than a bird's nest?

Animal Home Discussion Starter

Look at the picture of the inside of the squirrel's nest.
What can you learn about this squirrel by studying its nest?

Writing Ideas

1. A Report about a Squirrel's Nest
   a. Tell about who lives in this nest.
   b. Tell how a squirrel nest is built.
   c. Tell why this is a good home for a tree squirrel.

2. Sometimes squirrels build their nests in hollow trees.
   Pretend you are moving into a hollow tree.
   Describe what you would do to make it a comfortable place to live.

3. Compare a bird nest and a tree squirrel nest.

4. Write a story about a squirrel and its nest.

Getting Ready for Winter
Strange Things in the Squirrel's Nest
Noisy Squirrels in the Neighborhood

Gray Squirrel Nest

There are tree squirrels such as red, gray, and flying squirrels that live in woodland areas, often high up in trees. There are also ground squirrels which have shorter tails and never climb trees.

Gray squirrels live where there are trees. They are well adapted for living in trees. They use their sharp claws for clinging to the bark of trees. They use their fluffy tail to help keep their balance as they move along tree branches. Squirrels are able to leap through the trees easily.

Squirrels build bulky, ball-shaped nests in the forks of tree branches. Sometimes they build their nests in hollow tree trunks. The nests are made of twigs and leaves.

Squirrels rest and sleep in their nests. They use it to store nuts for winter. They also raise their babies in their nests.

Simple Science Reports

Gray Squirrel Nest

Inside the Gray Squirrel Nest

Simple Science Report
TRAP-DOOR SPIDER

Provide books and other materials about spiders and their homes for students reporting on trap-door spiders. (You may need to read these to younger students.) Discuss the information they have learned, then assign a writing task.

Outside and Inside Spiders by Sandra Markle; Bradbury, 1994
Trapdoor Spiders by L. Martin; Rourke Corp., 1988

Discussion Starters
Where do trap-door spiders build their traps?

What does the spider do to catch food in its trap?

What else does the trap-door spider use the tunnel for?

Can you think of other ways spiders trap food?

Why are spiders an important part of nature?

Animal Home Discussion Starter
Look carefully at the picture of the inside of the trap-door spider's tunnel.
Can you figure out what the trap-door spider uses to make the door?

Writing Ideas
1. A Report about a Trap-Door Spider
   a. Tell about who lives in this tunnel.
   b. Tell how a trap-door is built.
   c. Tell why this is a good home for a trap-door spider.

2. Describe the ways a spider uses its silk.

3. A trap-door spider makes a hinge on its door. List the places people use hinges.

4. Write a story about a trap-door spider.

Trapped in the Spider's Burrow
How to Catch Your Dinner by A. Spider
The Spider Who Ran Out of Silk

Trap-Door Spider

Spiders spin a kind of silk that looks very delicate, but is really very strong. This silk is used to trap food and to wrap around prey until it is eaten. The silk is used to make a sack that holds the spider's eggs until they hatch. Some spiders use the silk to spin webs of different types and some use it to line their homes.

Many types of tarantulas build underground burrows as homes. One type, the trap-door spider, adds a cover to its burrow. This is a very special door because it has a hinge.

Trap-door spiders use large spines which grow along their jaws to dig out the tunnel. They scrape away bits of earth, roll it into balls, and carry it outside the burrow. The spider uses saliva and earth to make the walls of the burrow smooth and firm. Then the spider lines the walls with silk.

The door is made out of a sturdy layer of silk. The spider continues the silk from the lining into the silk that makes the door to create a firm hinge. The outer surface of the door is covered with something natural to the area (moss, leaves, sticks, etc.) to camouflage it.

When the trap-door spider is ready to hunt, it pushes the door open and sits quietly until its prey crawls by. The trap-door spider reaches out, grabs its prey and moves quickly back into the tunnel. The spider grabs hold of the silk on the inside of the door and pulls the door shut.

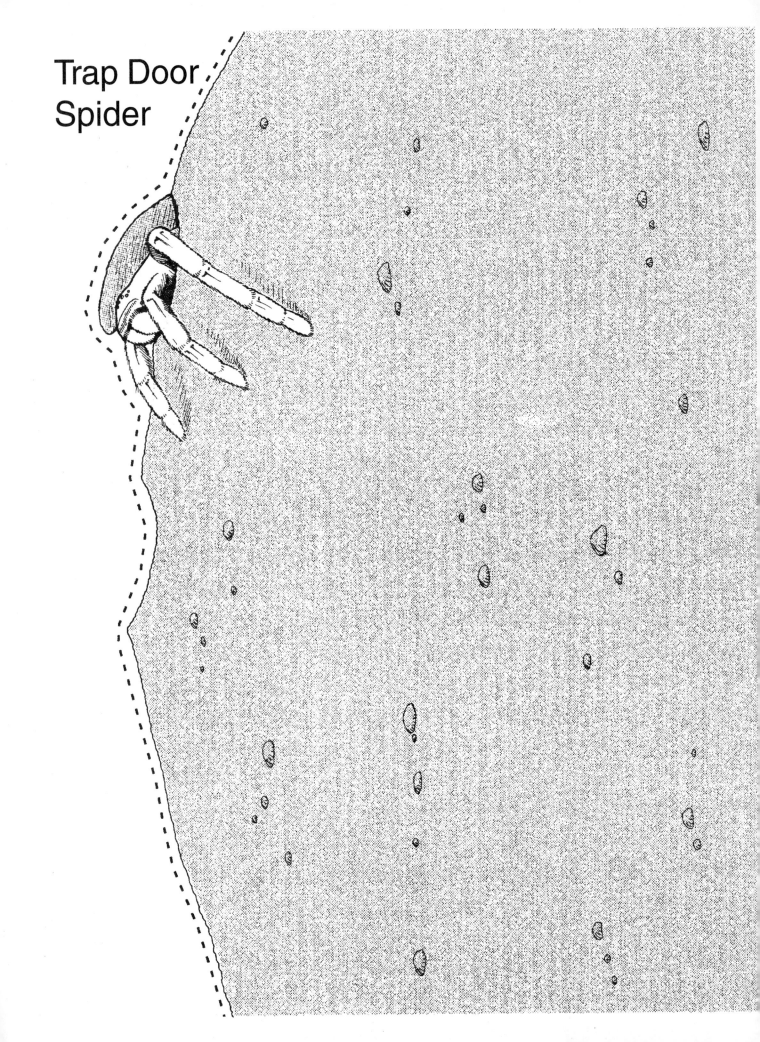

Trap Door
Spider

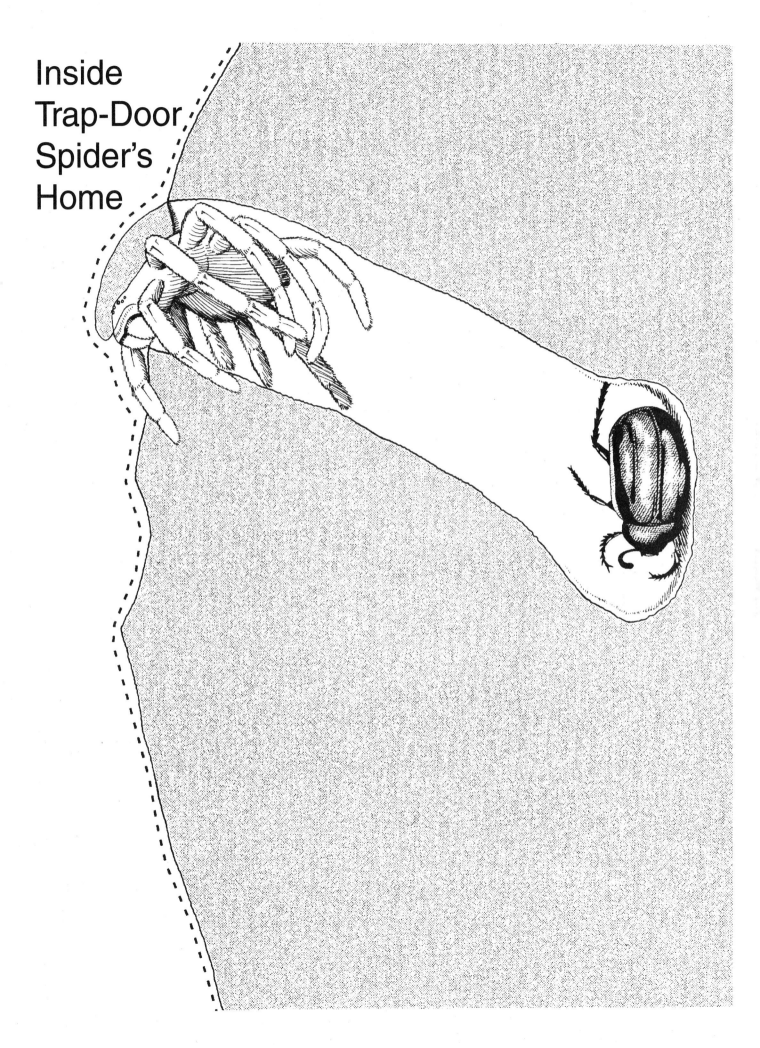

Inside
Trap-Door
Spider's
Home

Simple Science Report
RABBIT WARREN

Provide books and other materials about rabbits and their homes for students reporting on rabbit warrens. (You may need to read these to younger students.) Discuss the information they have learned, then assign a writing task.

The Rabbit in the Field by Jennifer Coldrey; Gareth Stevens, 1987
The World of Rabbits by Jennifer Coldrey; Stevens, 1987

Discussion Starters

What does a rabbit warren look like?

How do rabbits build their homes?

How does the warren help protect the rabbits?

How does the mother rabbit take care of her babies in the warren?

Do all kinds of rabbits live in warrens?

Animal Home Discussion Starter

Look at the picture of the inside of a rabbit warren.
What are some of the ways rabbits use the rooms in the warren?

Writing Ideas

1. A Report about a Rabbit Warren
   a. Tell about who lives in this warren.
   b. Tell how a warren is built.
   c. Tell why this is a good home for a rabbit.

2. Describe how a mother rabbit prepares her nest and takes care of her babies.

3. Not all rabbits live in warrens.
   Find out where other kinds of rabbits live.
   Write a description of how they live.

4. Write a story about a rabbit and its warren.

Life in Bunnyville
The Magician's Rabbit
Rabbits in Our Backyard

Rabbit Warren

Many kinds of wild rabbits make their homes in empty burrows left when another kind of animal leaves. Some make their homes in piles of brush or wild grasses. Other kinds of rabbits live underground in burrows and tunnels which they build. This rabbit home is called a warren.

Rabbits use their front paws to dig deep into the soil. They build tunnels just large enough for a rabbit to move through easily. The burrows are bigger than the tunnels and can be deep under the ground.

A rabbit warren usually has several entrances. It also has "bolt holes." These are small openings just big enough for the rabbit to squeeze through in an emergency.

The same warren may be used by families of rabbits for many years. A rabbit warren may be home to only a few rabbits or to more than a hundred.

The warren is where the rabbits sleep and where they raise their babies. A mother doe builds a nest in one of the burrows. She collects grass to line the nest. The burrow provides a safe place to be. She covers up the opening to the nest when she goes out to feed. This hides the nest from predators and it keeps the heat in the nest so the babies stay warm.

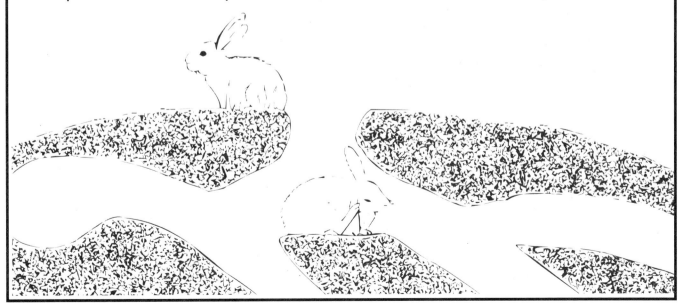

Rabbit Warren

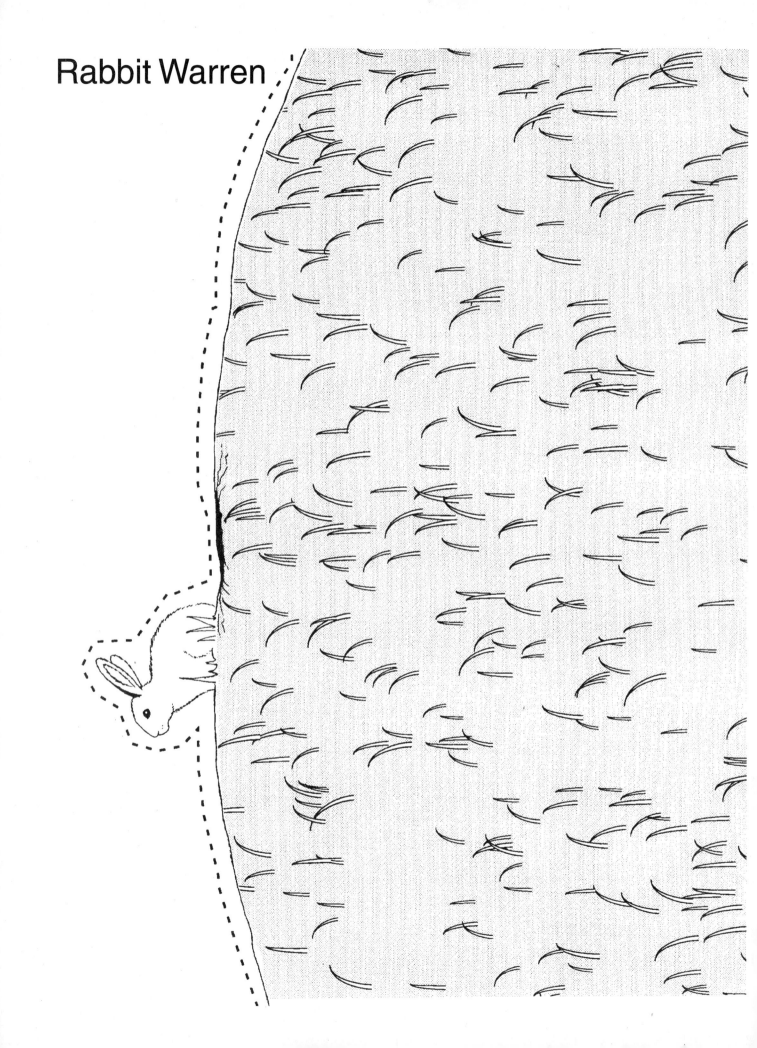

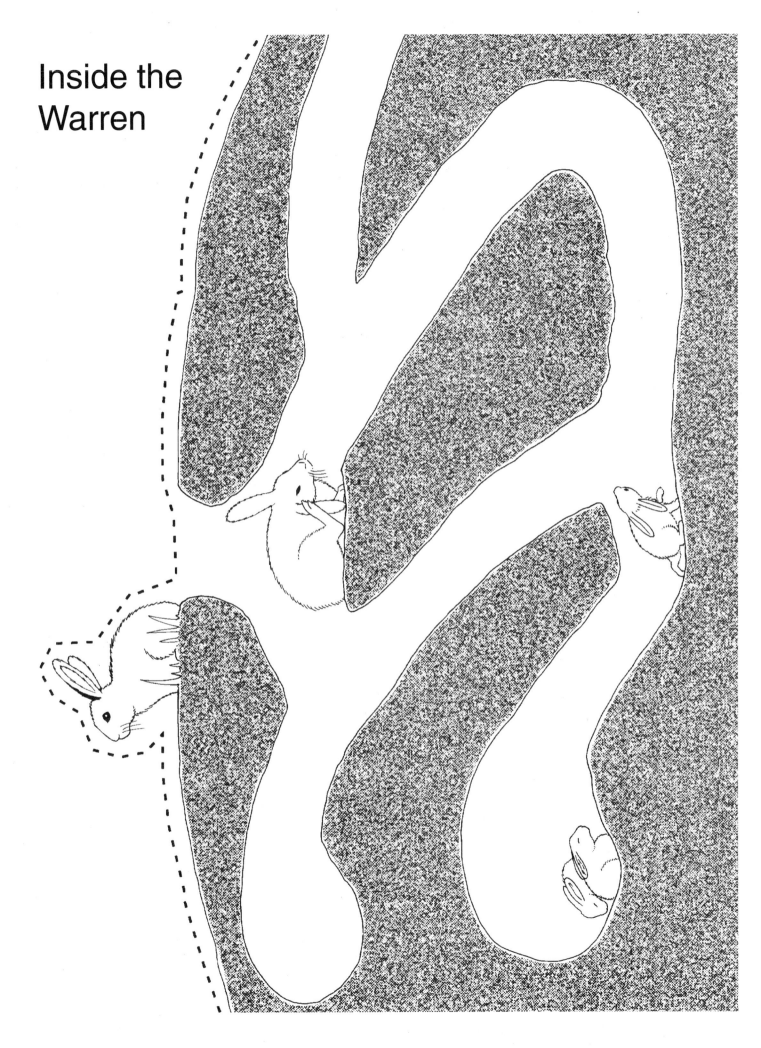

Inside the
Warren

Simple Science Report
POLAR BEAR DEN

Provide books and other materials about bears and their homes for students reporting on polar bears and their dens. (You may need to read these to younger students.) Discuss the information they have learned, then assign a writing task.

The World of the Polar Bears by Virginia Harrison; Gareth Stevens, 1989
Arctic Animals by Bobbie Kalman; Crabtree, 1988

Discussion Starters

What kind of den does the polar bear have?

Does the bear make the den?

How does the polar bear stay warm during the long winter?

What does it do for food?

How does the mother polar bear take care of her babies during the winter?

Animal Home Discussion Starter

Look at the picture of the inside of a polar bear's den.
What can you tell about the polar bear by studying the picture?

Writing Ideas

1. A Report about a Polar Bear's Den
   a. Tell about who lives in a den.
   b. Tell how a den is built.
   c. Tell why this is a good winter home for a polar bear.

2. Describe a polar bear's habitat.

3. A polar bear and a seal are both animals that live in the cold north.
   They are also both mammals. Tell how they are alike and how they are different.

4. Write a story about a polar bear and its den.

Oh, no! My Den is Melting
The Bear Who Couldn't Sleep
Baby Polar Bears

Polar Bear Den

Polar bears are built for living in the cold snow and ice. The soles of their feet are furry which helps them move across snow and ice without slipping. They have thick fur and a large layer of fat to keep their
bodies warm.

Polar bears hunt all year round, even in the cold winter. Most females stay in dens with their cubs for several months in the winter.

The mother polar bear digs a den in a snowdrift. She makes a "breathing hole" in the roof of the den to let in fresh air. Soon gusty winds and snowstorms will cover over the entrance.

The den makes a cozy and safe place for the polar bear to have her cubs. She usually has one or two cubs at a time. The cubs are tiny and helpless at first. She feeds them rich milk from her body and they grow big and strong.

The mother bear often digs an extra little room in the den. This is a "playroom" where the cubs can move around while mother sleeps the winter away.

Mother and her cubs stay in the den until spring arrives. She digs an opening out of the den using her powerful paws. Mother takes her cubs out into the wide-open spaces where they begin exploring their world.

The polar bear's job is not over. Now she must protect her cubs as she teaches them how to hunt and to live on their own.

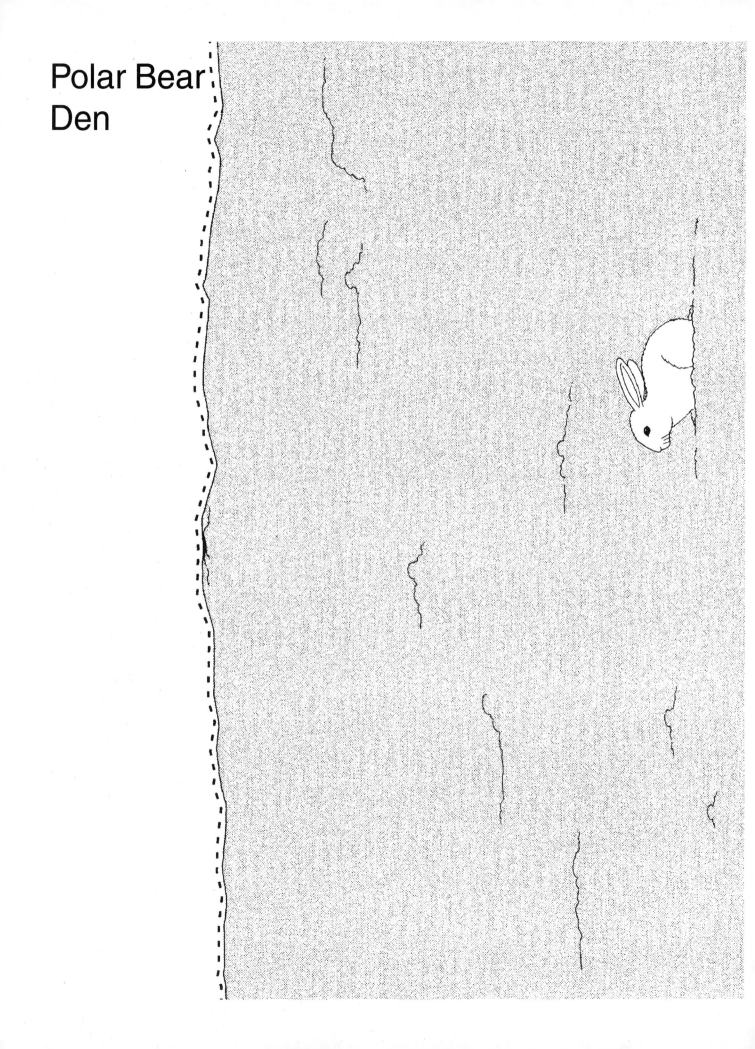

Polar Bear
Den

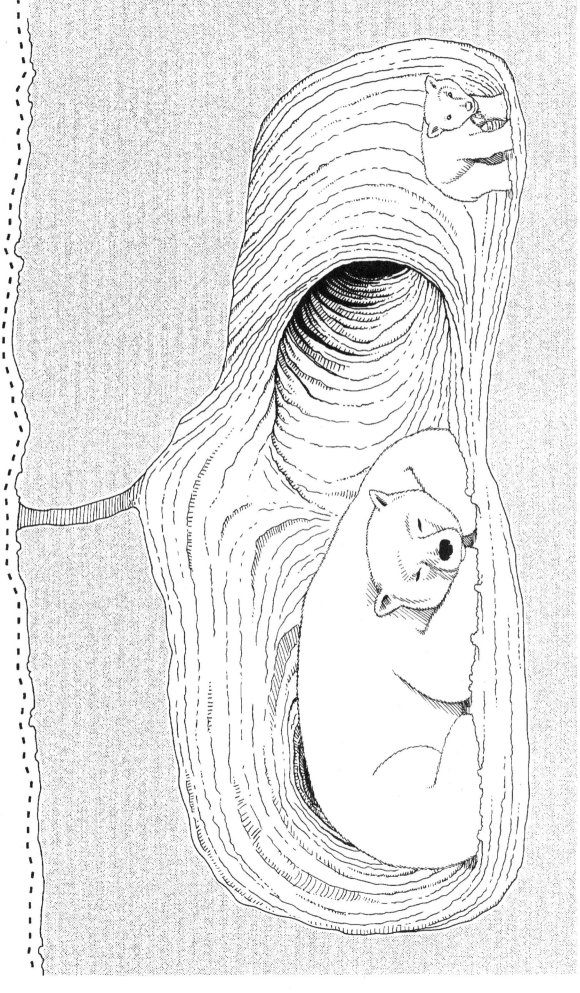

Inside
the Den

Simple Science Report
MOLEHILL

Provide books and other materials about moles and their homes for students reporting on molehills. (You may need to read these to younger students.) Discuss the information they have learned, then assign a writing task.

Mole's Hill: A Woodland Tale by Lois Ehlert; Harcourt, 1994

Discussion Starters
Where does a mole live?

How does it make its home?

Does the mole have any special parts to help it build its home?

What does a mole eat?

How does a mole find its food?

Is this destructive or helpful?

Animal Home Discussion Starter
Look at the picture of the inside of the molehill.
How are the different parts of the mole's home used?

Writing Ideas
1. A Report about a Molehill
   a. Tell about who lives in a molehill.
   b. Tell how a molehill is built.
   c. Tell why this is a good home for a mole.

2. Think about how a mole builds its tunnels and about what moles eat.
   Tell how the mole would be helpful and how it would be harmful in a garden.

3. A mole uses its strong sense of smell to find food.
   Describe how you use your nose, eyes, and ears to find your food.

4. Write a story about a mole and its molehill.

   Mole's Adventure
   Life in a Molehill
   How to Catch a Mole Without Hurting It

Molehill

Moles are small rodents living in woods, fields, and sometimes in our backyards and gardens. They build tunnels underground. The tunnels are where they live and search for food.

Moles have broad front paws with strong claws. These claws work like shovels as the mole digs its tunnels in the earth. The molehill we see in our yards and gardens is made from the soil the mole pushes out of the way as it digs.

Moles dig two kinds of tunnels. There are tunnels deep under the ground where the mole lives. There are tunnels just under the surface of the ground where moles look for food. The mole digs new tunnels every day as it searches for food.

The mole digs a large burrow deep under the ground. This is where the mole rests and raises its young. A nest of grass and leaves is built in one "room" for the babies. A separate room is used to store worms and insects until they are eaten by the mole.

A mole does not have very good eyesight, but it has a very good sense of smell. It uses this sense of smell to find worms and insects in the dark tunnels. Moles have fur that stands straight up. This way the hair bends in whatever direction the mole is going. They have special hairs on their front feet and tails. These help keep the mole from bumping into tunnel walls as they move around.

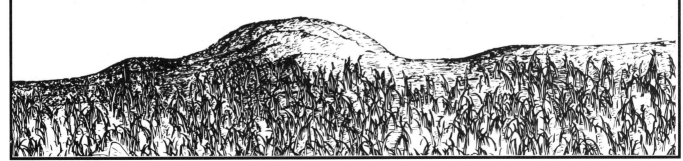

Molehill

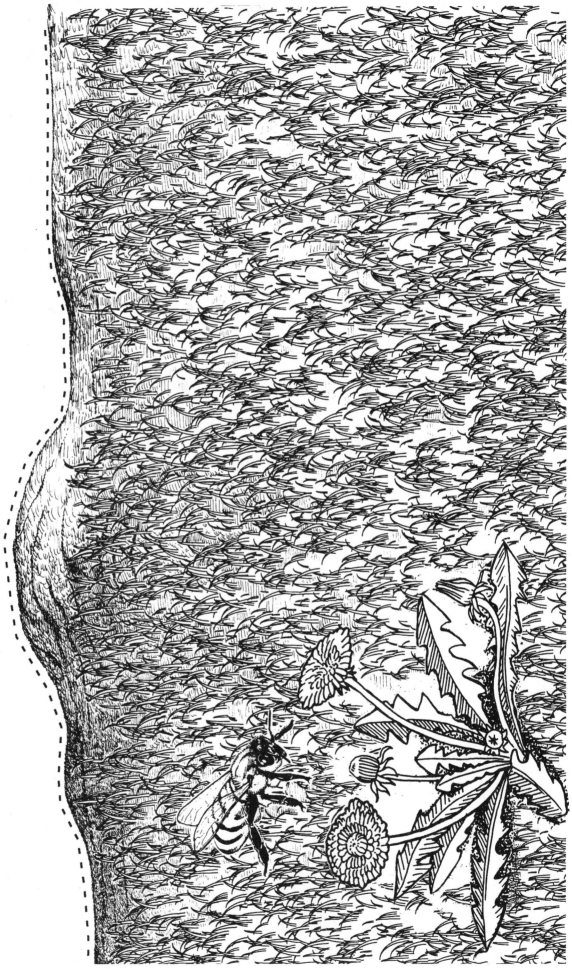

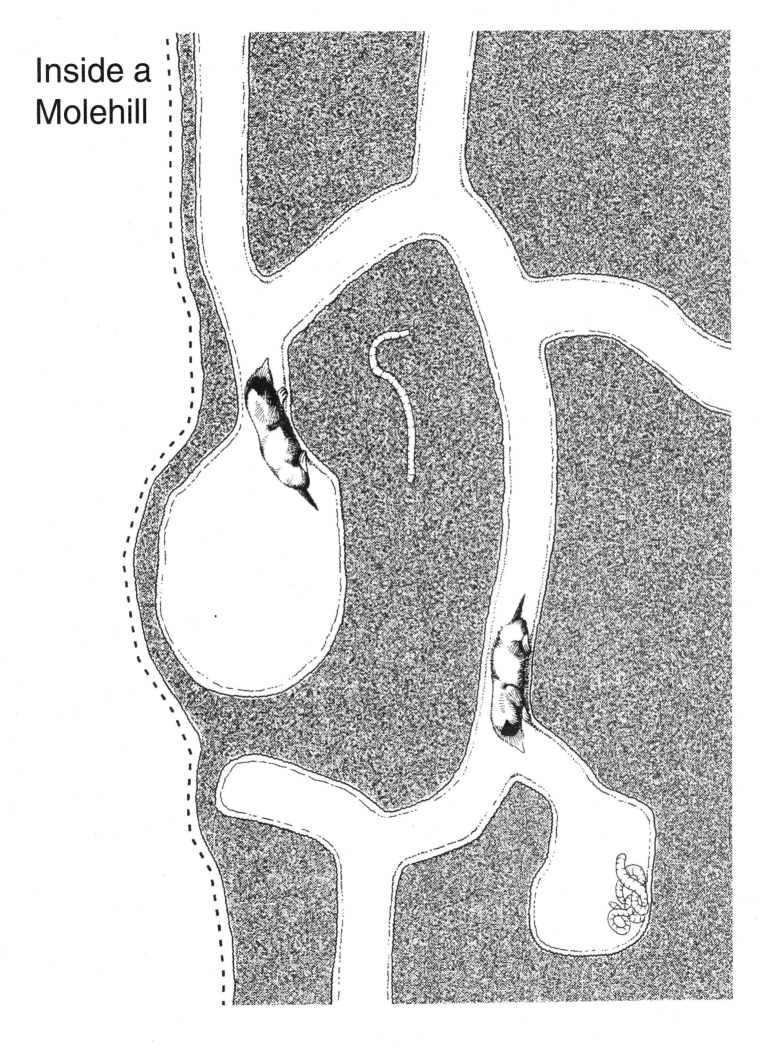

Inside a
Molehill

Simple Science Report
ELF OWL HOLE

Provide books and other materials about owls and their homes for students reporting on elf owl hole. (You may need to read these to younger students.) Discuss the information they have learned, then assign a writing task.

Discussion Starters

What is unusual about the elf owl's home?

How is the elf owl's hole made?

When do owls hunt for food?

What do they eat?

How do they find their food?

Animal Home Discussion Starter

Look at the picture of the inside of the elf owl's hole.
Can you think of some reasons why this is a good home for a tiny owl?

Writing Ideas

1. A Report about an Elf Owl's Hole
    a. Tell about who lives in the hole.
    b. Tell how an elf owl's hole is built.
    c. Tell why this is a good home for a little elf owl.

2. Describe one way the clever elf owl catches its food.

3. Elf owls are birds. Make a list of all the birds you can name.

4. Write a story about an elf owl and its home.

> **The Little Owl Who Was Afraid of the Dark**
> **Two Eggs in the Nest**
> **Elf Owl's Great Adventure**

Elf Owl Hole

Owls live all over the world except in the cold Antarctic. The elf owl lives in hot deserts.

Elf owls are one of the smallest owls in the world. During the day, it roosts in a tree or bush and comes out at dusk to hunt insects and scorpions.

Elf owls nest in empty woodpecker holes in cactus plants or tree trunks. When the male elf owl finds a good hole, he sings to attract a female and get her to enter the nest. In the spring she lays from one to five tiny eggs. The male feeds the female while she sits on the eggs. He also brings food for her to give to the young owlets when they
are hatched.

Elf owls are smart hunters. An elf owl will grab the stalk of a plant and hang upside down from it. Then the elf owl beats its wings to make the stalk shake. Any insects resting on the stalk run or fly out and are caught by the hungry owl.

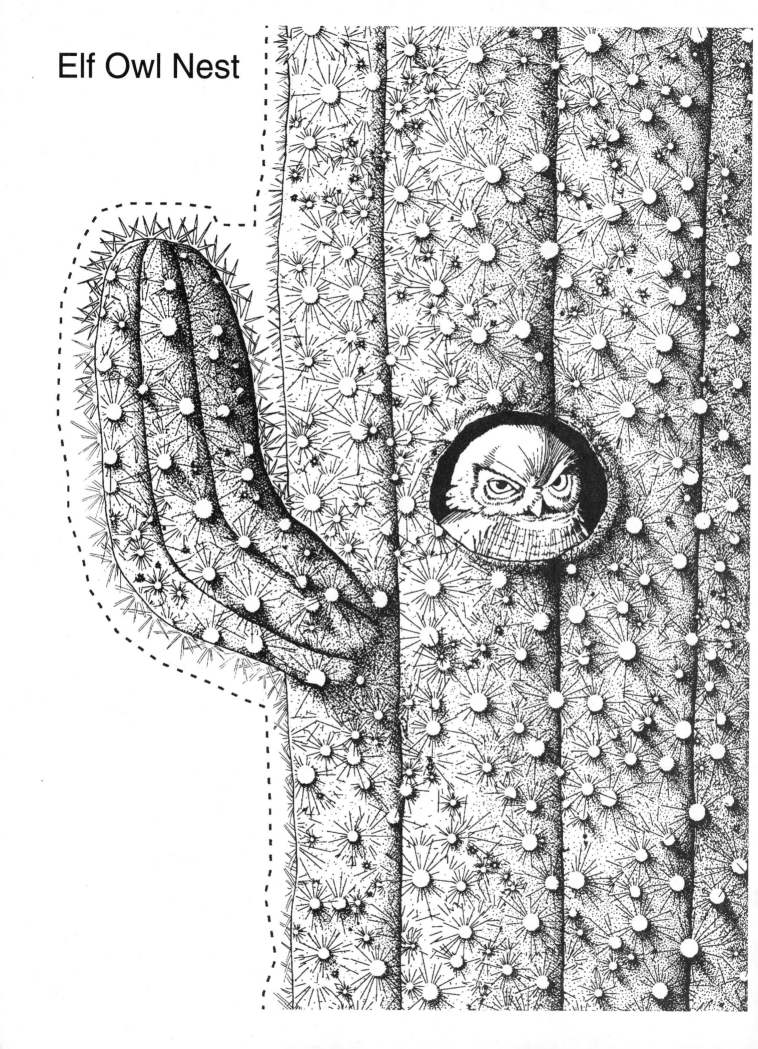

Elf Owl Nest

Inside the Elf Owl Nest

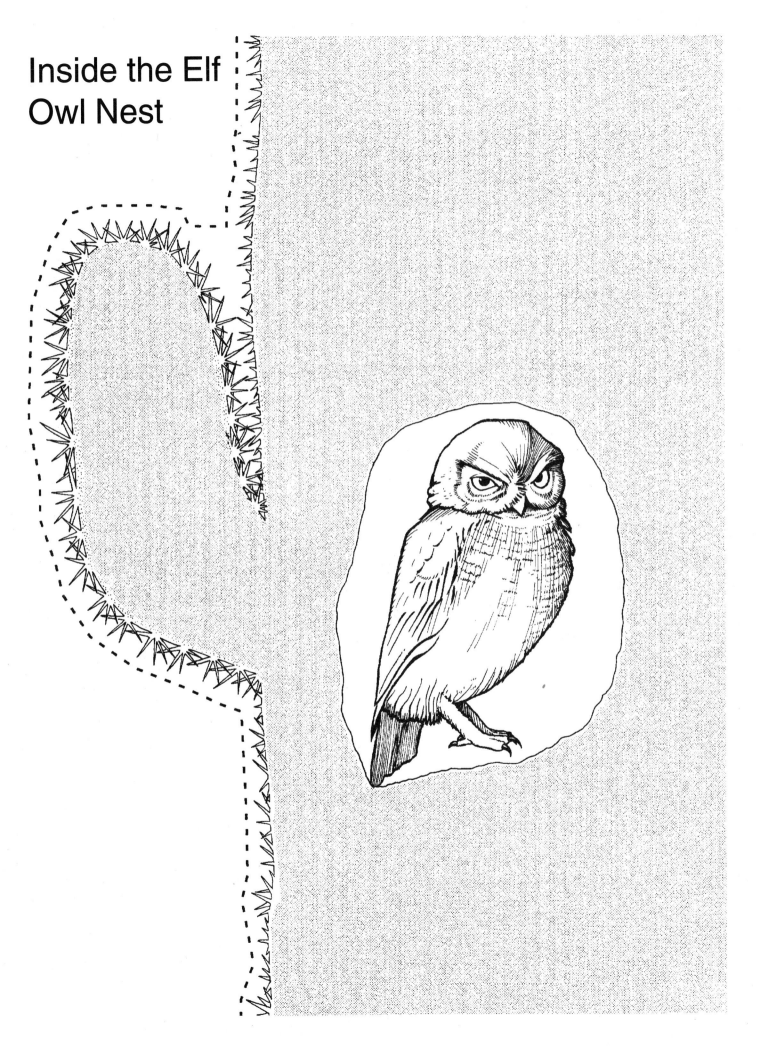

Simple Science Report
PRAIRIE DOG TOWN

Provide books and other materials about prairie dogs and their homes for students reporting on prairie dog towns. (You may need to read these to younger students.) Discuss the information they have learned, then assign a writing task.

Prairie Dogs by Lynn Stone; Rourke corp., 1993
Prairie Dog Town by Janette Oke; Bethel Pub., 1988

Discussion Starters

What is a prairie dog?

What are the parts of a prairie dog town called?

What are the different areas used for?

How do prairie dogs warn each other of danger?

Why do you think this is called a "town"?

Animal Home Discussion Starter

Look at the picture of the inside of the prairie dog's home.
Do you think this is a whole prairie dog town or the home for one prairie dog family?
Why do you think so?

Writing Ideas

1. A Report about a Prairie Dog Town
   a. Tell about who lives in this "town."
   b. Tell how a prairie dog town is built.
   c. Tell why this is a good home for prairie dogs.

2. Compare a prairie dog with a real dog. How are they alike? How are they different?

3. Describe how prairie dogs guard their town.

4. Write a story about a prairie dog and its town.

A Prairie Dog Party
How to Dig a Tunnel
If I Were a Prairie Dog

Prairie Dog Town

Prairie dogs are related to ground squirrels. They like to live together in small family groups. Many families live near each other in colonies or towns. The towns are made up of many tunnels connected to each other under the ground. Some prairie dog towns cover more than 100 acres (10 hectares).

Low mounds of dirt or sand are piled around the openings to the tunnels. Prairie dog "guards" sit upright on these mounds and watch for danger. If danger comes, the guard gives a sharp whistle to warn the other prairie dogs. They all hurry down into the tunnels for safety.

Prairie dogs eat grass and other green plants. They have chisel-like front teeth that help them eat these plants.

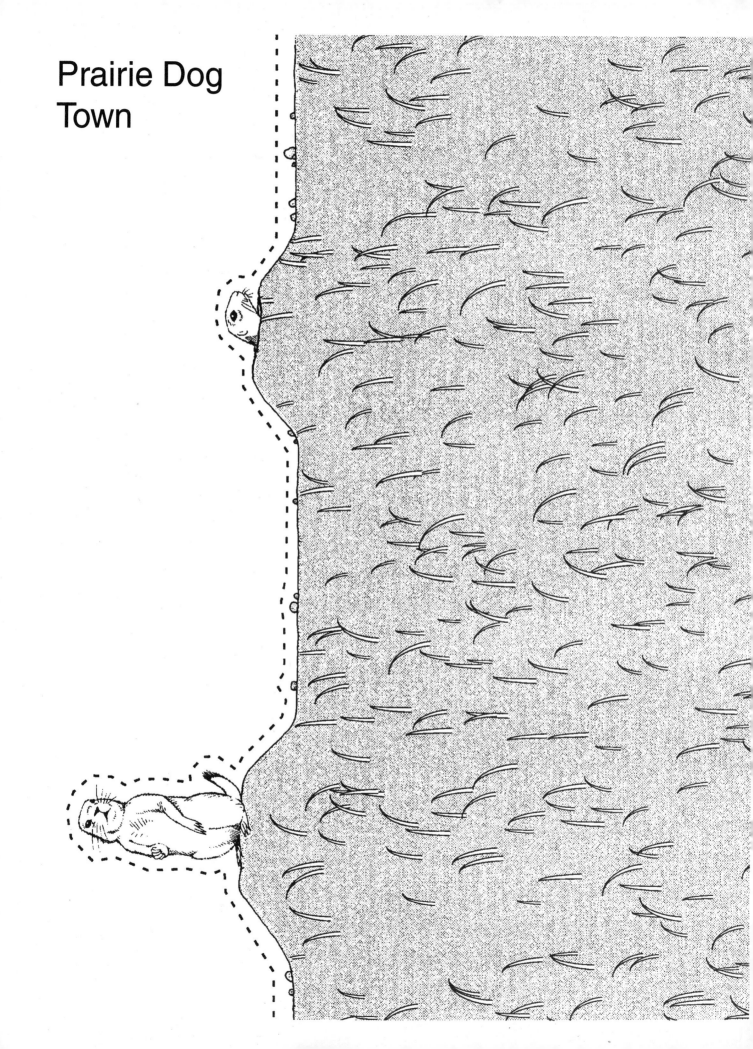

Prairie Dog
Town

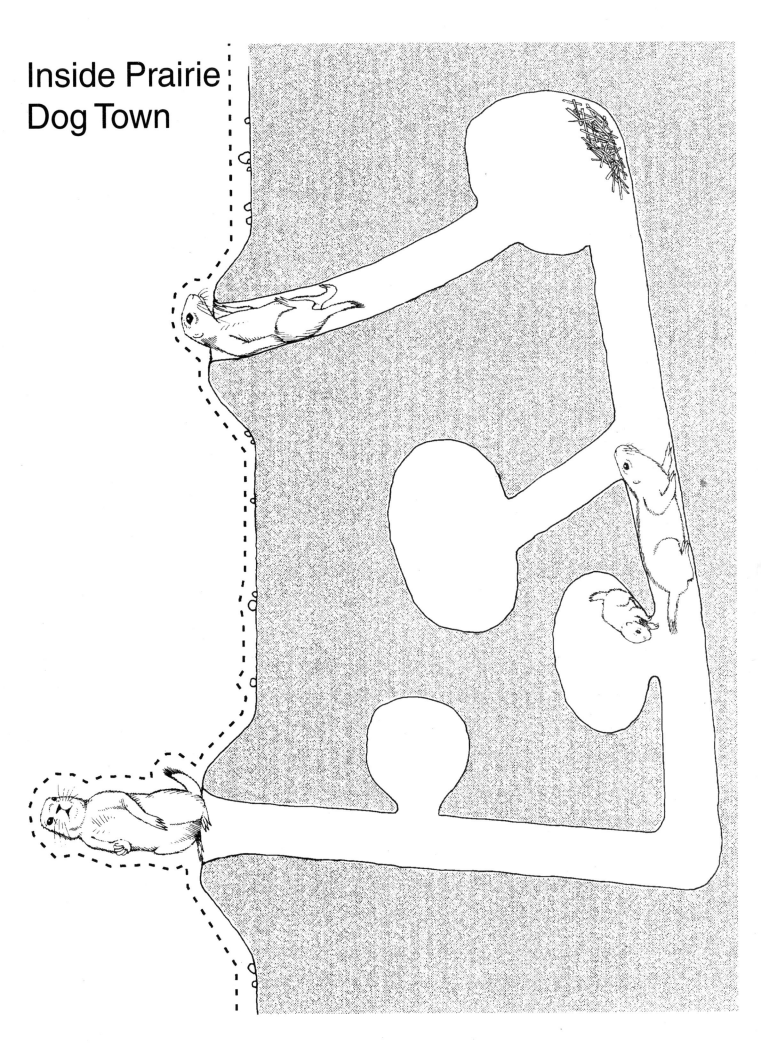

Inside Prairie Dog Town

Simple Science Reports

Part III
PREHISTORIC ANIMALS

Contents

Bibliography

The Big Beast Book by Jerry Booth; Yolla Bolly Press, 1988

Dinosaurs by Gail Gibbons; Holiday House, 1987

Dinosaur Encore by Patricia Mullins; Harper Collins/Perlman, 1993

Dinosaurs of North America by Helen Roney Sattler; Lothrop,
    Lee & Shepard, 1981

Dougal Dixon's Dinosaurs by Dougal Dixon; Boyds Mills Press, 1993

How Big Were the Dinosaurs? by Bernard Most; Harcourt Brace
    and Co., 1994

My Visit to the Dinosaurs by Aliki; Harper and Row, 1969

Tyrannosaurus Rex and Its Kin: The Mesozoic Monsters by Helen
    Roney Sattler; Lothrop, Lee & Shepard, 1989

What Color is That Dinosaur? Questions, Answers, and Mysteries by
    Lowell Dingus; Millbrook, 1994

Simple Science Report
STEGOSAURUS

Provide books and other materials about the stegosaurus for students reporting on this dinosaur. (You may need to read these to younger students.) Discuss the information they have learned, then assign a writing task.

Stegosaurs: The Solar-powered Dinosaurs by Helen Roney Sattler; Lothrop, Lee & Shepard, 1992
Stegosaurus by Angela Sheehan; Ray Rourke Publishing Co., 1981

Discussion Starters
How would you describe a stegosaurus?

How could its "plates" help stegosaurus?

What did stegosaurus probably eat?

How did it get its food?

Skeleton Discussion Starter
Look at the skeleton of the stegosaurus.
Can you find the part of stegosaurus that was used for defense?

Writing Ideas
1. A Report about a Stegosaurus
   a. Tell what a stegosaurus looked like.
   b. Tell what a stegosaurus ate.
   c. Tell how a stegosaurus got its food.

2. Describe how a stegosaurus' body helped protect it from predators.

3. Explain how scientists can tell what a stegosaurus ate.

4. Write a story about a stegosaurus.

A Day in the Life of Stegosaurus
If I Met a Stegosaurus
Discovering Dinosaur Bones

Stegosaurus

Stegosaurus was the only dinosaur in North America that had plates. Stegosaurus fossils have been found in Europe also.

Stegosaurus had a body about the size of an elephant. It was about 11 feet (3.3 meters) tall at the hips and 25 feet (7.5 meters) long.

The stegosaurus had two rows of leaf-shaped bony plates running down its back and onto its tail. No one knows exactly what the plates were for. Some scientists think they may have helped regulate stegosaurus' temperature. The long, heavy tail had four large spikes. In fact, each spike was about 1 foot (30 centimeters) long. This spiky tail made a great weapon.

Stegosaurus had short front legs and long back legs. It walked on all four legs, but could rear up on its hind legs to feed in the trees. Even though it had a big body, the stegosaurus had a small head with a tiny brain. The head was carried low to the ground.

Stegosaurus' teeth show that it was a plant-eater. It had beak-like jaws and flat teeth for grinding tough leaves and stems. This peaceful plant eater probably grazed on ferns, horsetails, and other low-growing plants.

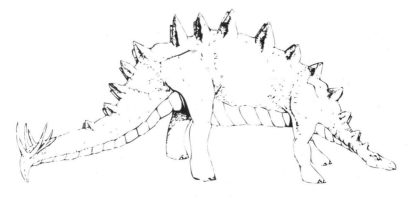

Stegosaurus

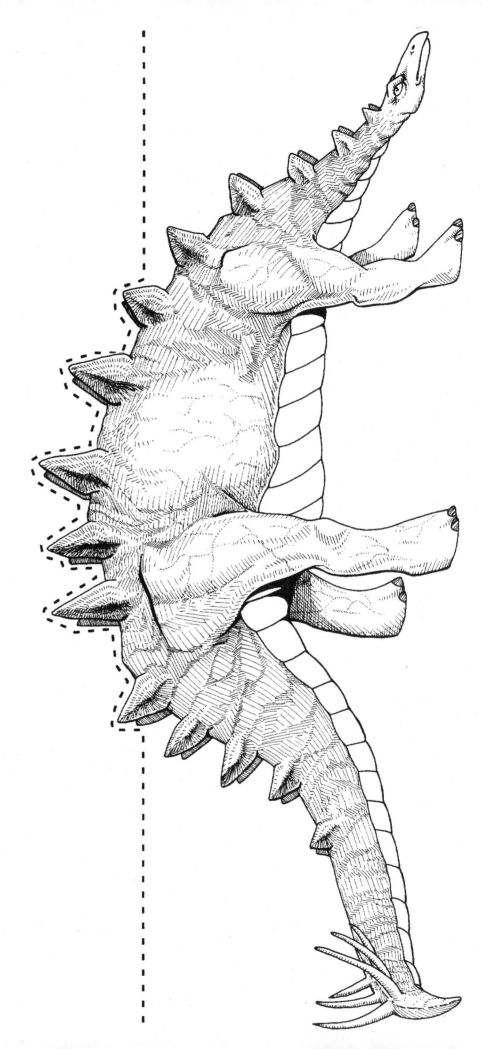

Stegasaurus Skeleton

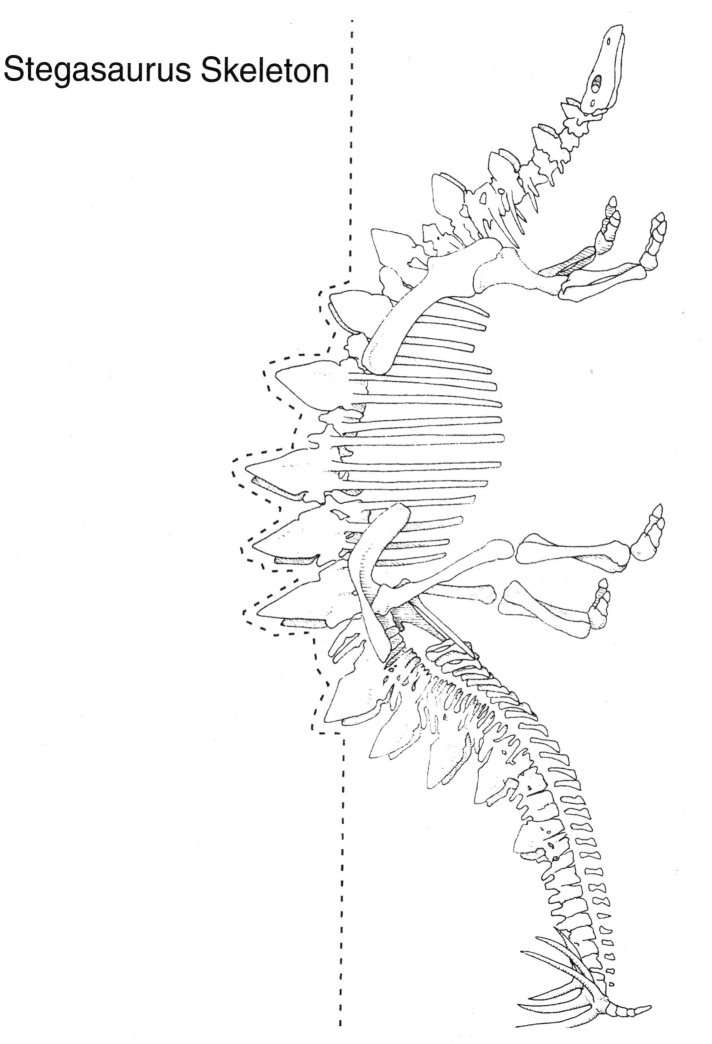

Simple Science Report
COMPSOGNATHUS

Provide books and other materials about the compsognathus for students reporting on this dinosaur. (You may need to read these to younger students.) Discuss the information they have learned, then assign a writing task.

Discussion Starters

How would you describe compsognathus?

What kind of meat did compsognathus probably eat?

How could a dinosaur this small protect itself?

Skeleton Discussion Starter

Look at the skeleton of the compsognathus. Can you tell if compsognathus was a big dinosaur or a small dinosaur by looking carefully at the bones in this picture? Why or why not?

Writing Ideas

1. A Report about a Compsognathus
    a. Tell what a compsognathus looked like.
    b. Tell what a compsognathus ate.
    c. Tell how a compsognathus got its food.

2. List the ways compsognathus was like a bird.

3. Compare little compsognathus with gigantic tyrannosaurus. How were they the same? How were they different?

4. Write a story about a compsognathus.

Strange Footprints in My Backyard
The Littlest Dinosaur
If I Were as Small as Compsognathus

Compsognathus

Do you think of huge creatures when someone mentions dinosaurs? Well, they were not all big. In fact, compsognathus was one of the smallest dinosaurs. It was about the size of a chicken.

Compsognathus moved along quickly on two long, delicate, bird-like legs. It had a small, pointed head and a long flexible neck. It had hollow bones like most modern birds. It may even have had feathers.

Compsognathus was a fast and deadly hunter. A compsognathus had sharp teeth. Its short arms had two-fingered hands with which it could catch and hold prey. It probably ate insects and small reptiles or mouse-like mammals.

Compsognathus

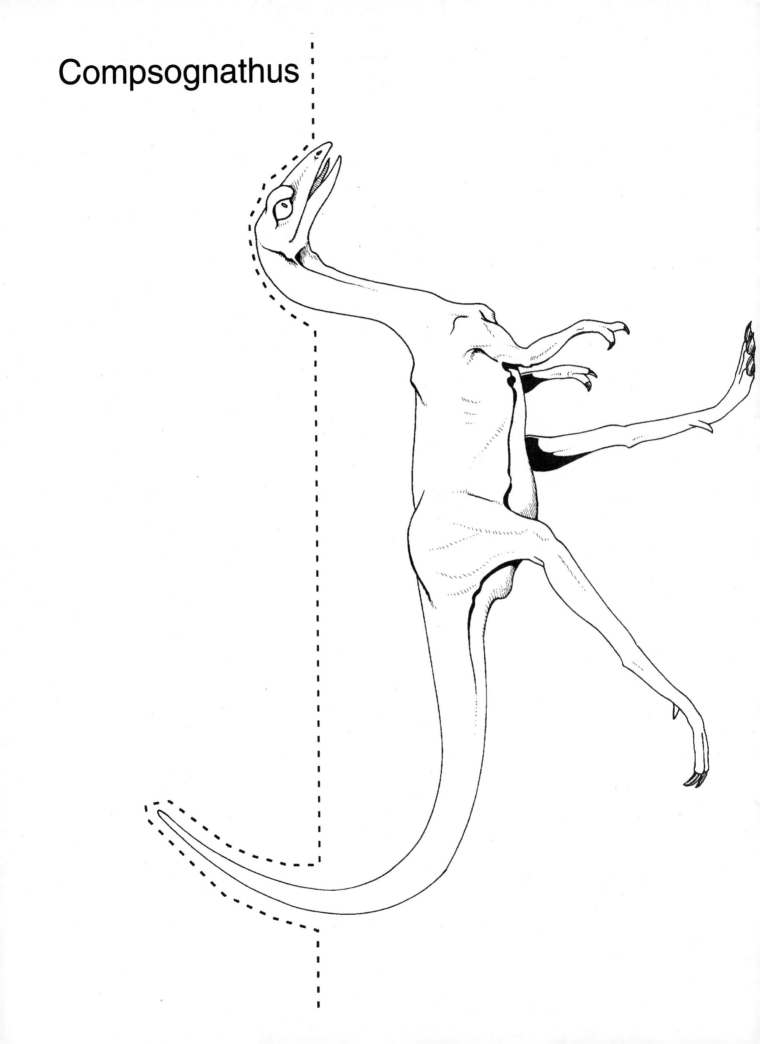

Compsognathus
Skeleton

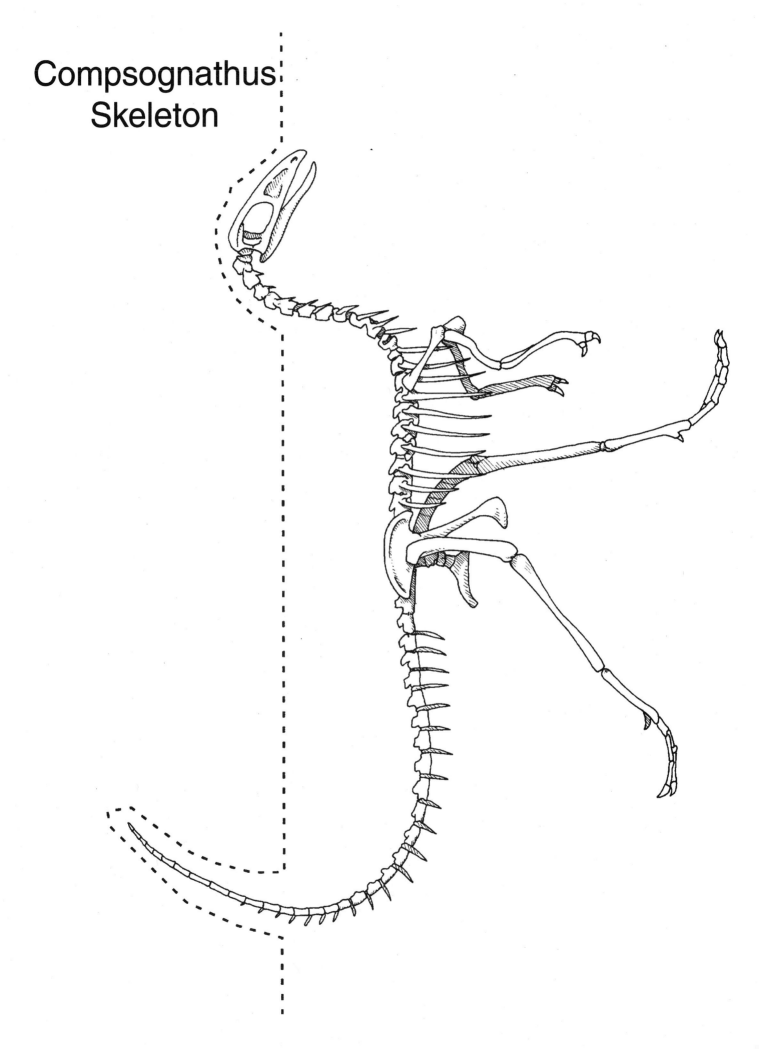

Simple Science Report
ARCHAEOPTERYX

Provide books and other materials about the archaeopteryx for students reporting on this prehistoric animal. (You may need to read these to younger students.) Discuss the information they have learned, then assign a writing task.

Archaeopteryx by Rupert Oliver; Rourke Enterprises, 1984

Discussion Starters
How would you describe archaeopteryx?

Could it fly or not?

What was the purpose of its feathers?

Skeleton Discussion Starter
Look at the picture of the archaeopteryx's skeleton.
In what ways was archaeopteryx like a modern bird?

Writing Ideas
1. A Report about an Archaeopteryx
   a. Tell what an archaeopteryx looked like.
   b. Tell what an archaeopteryx ate.
   c. Tell how an archaeopteryx moved.

2. List the ways archaeopteryx was like a dinosaur.

3. Compare archaeopteryx with a modern bird. How are they alike? How are they different?

4. Write a story about an archaeopteryx.

My First Flight
What Good are Feathers Anyway?
How to Catch a Tasty Bug

Archaeopteryx

Archaeopteryx was not a dinosaur. It is the oldest known bird. Its fossils show clear impressions of its feathers. Several archaeopteryx fossils have been found in West Germany.

Archaeopteryx looked a lot like a tiny dinosaur with feathers and wings. It was the size of a crow. It had a reptile-like skull and sharp teeth. Its bones were small and fragile. It had a long, bony tail and long, strong legs. Its wings were a lot like dinosaur arms. Both the tail and wings had long feathers. It had three clawed fingers on the front of each wing. Archaeopteryx probably ate insects.

Scientists disagree on how archaeopteryx moved. Some think it could fly, but not very far. Some think its wing muscles were too weak for it to take off from the ground to fly, but that it could have glided off of tree branches. Some think its strong legs were built for running on the ground and the feathers were for warmth, not flying. What do you think?

Archaeopteryx

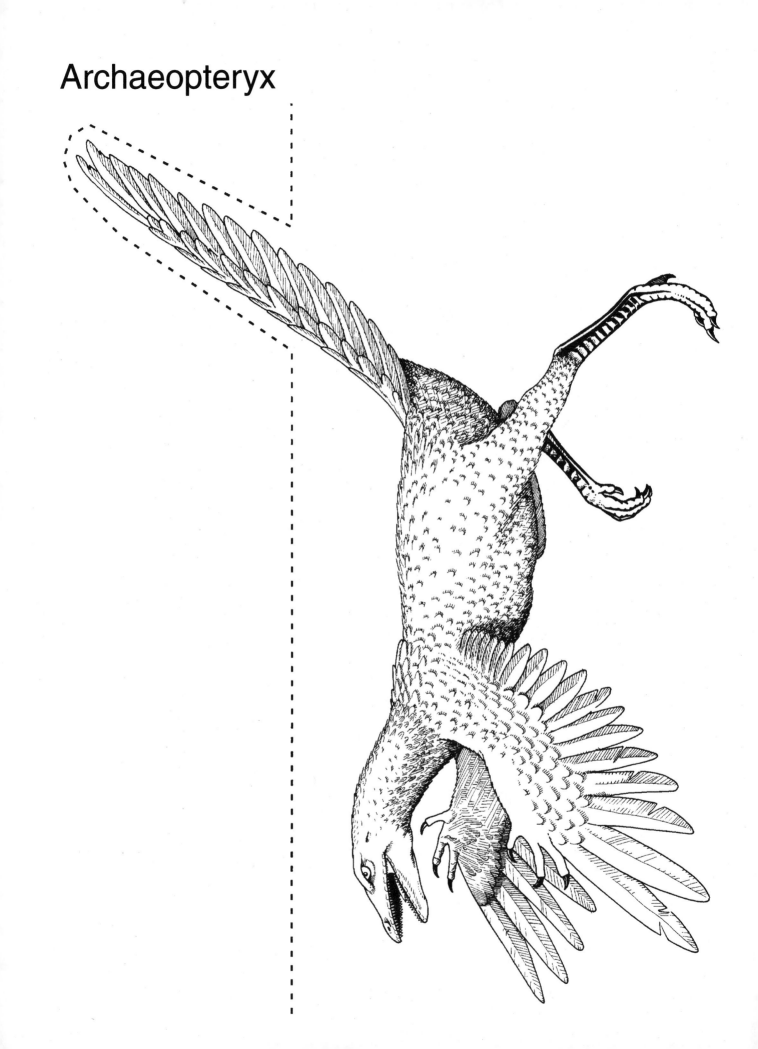

Archaeopteryx
Skeleton

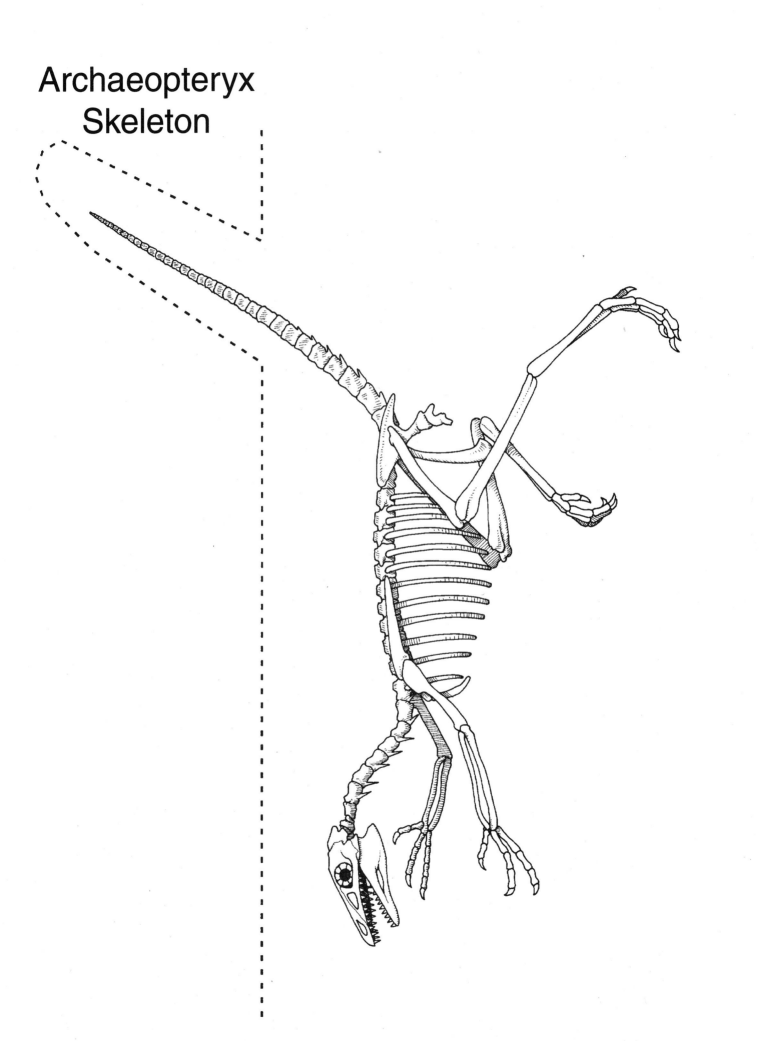

Simple Science Report
TYRANNOSAURUS

Provide books and other materials about the tyrannosaurus for students reporting on this dinosaur. (You may need to read these to younger students.) Discuss the information they have learned, then assign a writing task.

Tyrannosaurus by William Lindsay; Dorling Kindersley, 1992
Digging Up Tyrannosaurus Rex by John Horner; Crown, 1992
Tyrannosaurus by Angela Sheehan; Ray Rourke Publishing Co., 1981

Discussion Starters

How would you describe tyrannosaurus?

What did tyrannosaurs eat?

How did it get its food?

What does tyrannosaurus mean?

Skeleton Discussion Starter

Look at the skeleton of the tyrannosaurus.
Compare the front legs and the back legs.
Which were most useful to a tyrannosaurus?

Writing Ideas:

1. A Report about a Tyrannosaurus
   a. Tell what a tyrannosaurus looked like.
   b. Tell what a tyrannosaurus ate.
   c. Tell how a tyrannosaurus got its food.

2. What do <u>you</u> think the tyrannosaurus did with its short arms?

3. Describe how a meat-eating dinosaur such as tyrannosaurus was different than the plant-eating dinosaurs.

4. Write a story about a tyrannosaurus.

The Day I Met a Tyrannosaurus
How to Escape a Hungry Tyrannosaurus
The Timid Tyrannosaurus

Tyrannosaurus

Tyrannosaurus was a huge meat-eating dinosaur. It was 50 feet (15 meters) long from the tip of its enormous jaws to the end of its tail. It was 18.5 feet (5.6 meters) tall and weighed 6 tons (5.5 metric tons).

When it ran, tyrannosaurus held its tail out to balance its huge head. Its large jaws were lined with many six-inch (15 centimeter) -long saber-like teeth. Each of the teeth had serrated edges along the sides.

As if all those teeth were not enough of a weapon for a hungry tyrannosaurus, its huge feet had 8-inch (20 centimeter) -long claws.

Tyrannosaurus had long, strong hind legs, but its arms were very short. Although the arms were less than a yard (meter) long, they had long claws. Scientists don't know what these short arms were good for. One idea is that they helped the dinosaur get up from a lying-down position.

Tyrannosaurus was big, but not very fast moving. It stalked young duckbills or other prey that was easy to catch. It used its powerful jaws and sharp talons to capture and kill its prey.

Tyrannosaurus

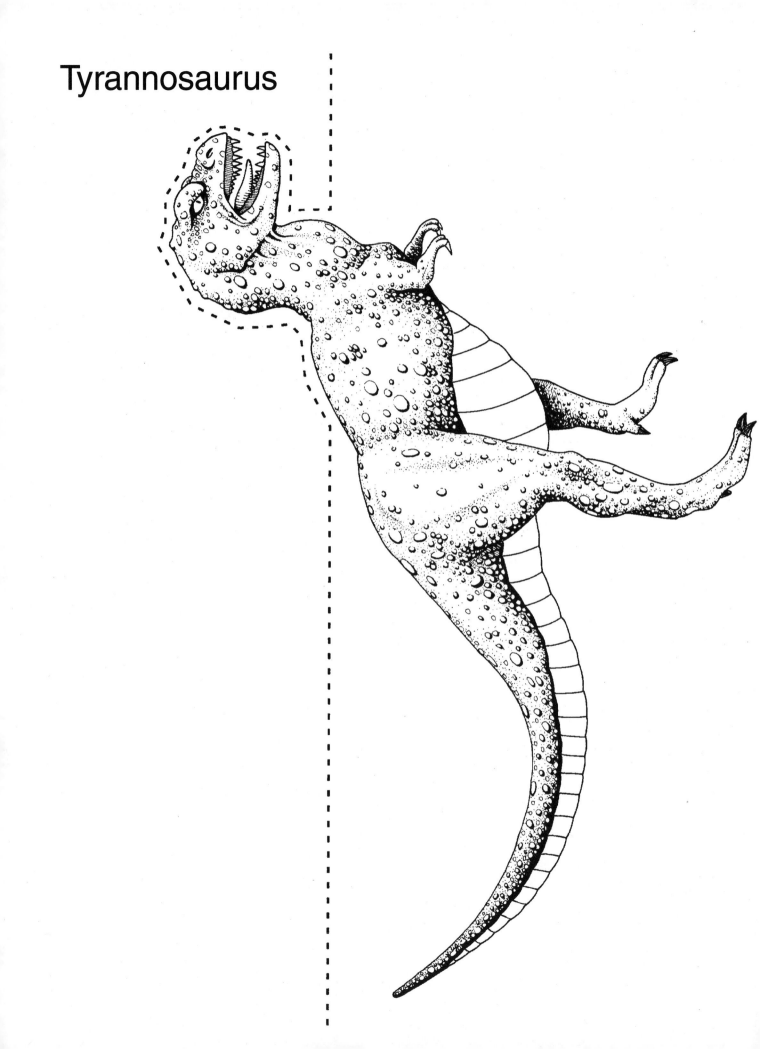

Tyrannosaurus Skeleton

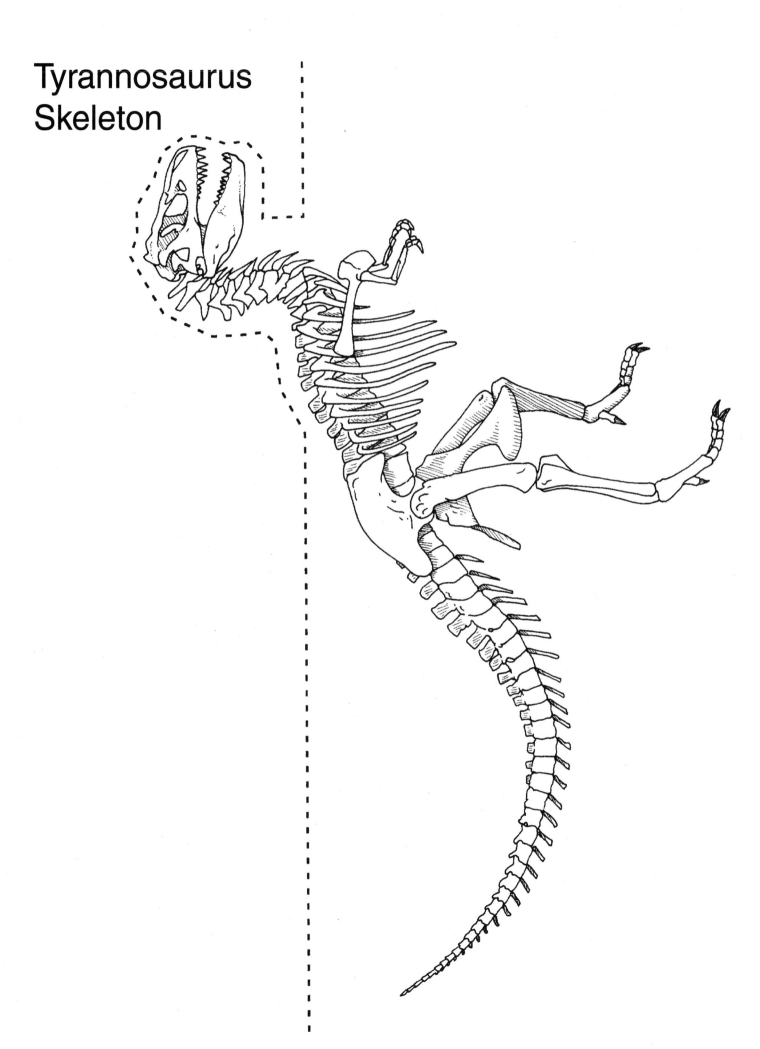

Simple Science Report
WOOLLY MAMMOTH

Provide books and other materials about the woolly mammoth for students reporting on this prehistoric animal. (You may need to read these to younger students.) Discuss the information they have learned, then assign a writing task.

Gone Forever by William Sanford and Carl Green; Crestwood House, 1989
Mike's Mammoth by Roy Gerrard; Farrar, Straus & Giroux, 1990
Woolly Mammoth by Ron Wilson; Rourke Enterprises, 1984

Discussion Starters

How would you describe the woolly mammoth?

Why did it need a long, woolly coat?

How was the woolly mammoth used by prehistoric man?

Which modern animal is the most like the woolly mammoth?

Skeleton Discussion Starter

Look at the skeleton of the woolly mammoth. How many different bones in this skeleton can you name?

Writing Ideas

1. A Report about a Woolly Mammoth
   a. Tell what a woolly mammoth looked like.
   b. Tell what a woolly mammoth ate.
   c. Tell how a woolly mammoth got its food.

2. Compare the woolly mammoth and a modern elephant.
   How are they alike? How are they different?

3. Explain how woolly mammoths could live in the cold of the Ice Age.

4. Write a story about a woolly mammoth.

   A Woolly Mammoth Hunt
   My Pet Woolly Mammoth
   In the News - A Frozen Woolly Mammoth is Found

Woolly Mammoth

Twenty thousand years ago much of earth was covered with ice and snow. It was called the Ice Age. Animals that looked like huge, shaggy elephants lived in the northern parts of Asia, North America, and Europe. These animals were called woolly mammoths.

Woolly mammoths were almost as big as modern elephants. They were covered with long, shaggy hair. This coat of shaggy hair, plus a layer of fat, kept the woolly mammoth warm through the long, cold days and nights.

Even though the earth was covered with a coat of ice, plants did grow. The woolly mammoth probably used its long tusks to clear away the snow from the ground to find ground plants to eat. It also ate the leaves from trees and bushes.

Scientists can only make an educated guess at what dinosaurs look like, but they know for sure what woolly mammoths looked like. They have found whole woolly mammoths frozen in the ice. The ice kept the mammoths from rotting, just like your freezer keeps meat fresh.

Woolly mammoths didn't live at the time of the dinosaurs. They lived at the same time as prehistoric man. These ancient men hunted the woolly mammoth. Think about how much meat one successful hunt could have provided these hungry hunters.

Woolly
Mammoth

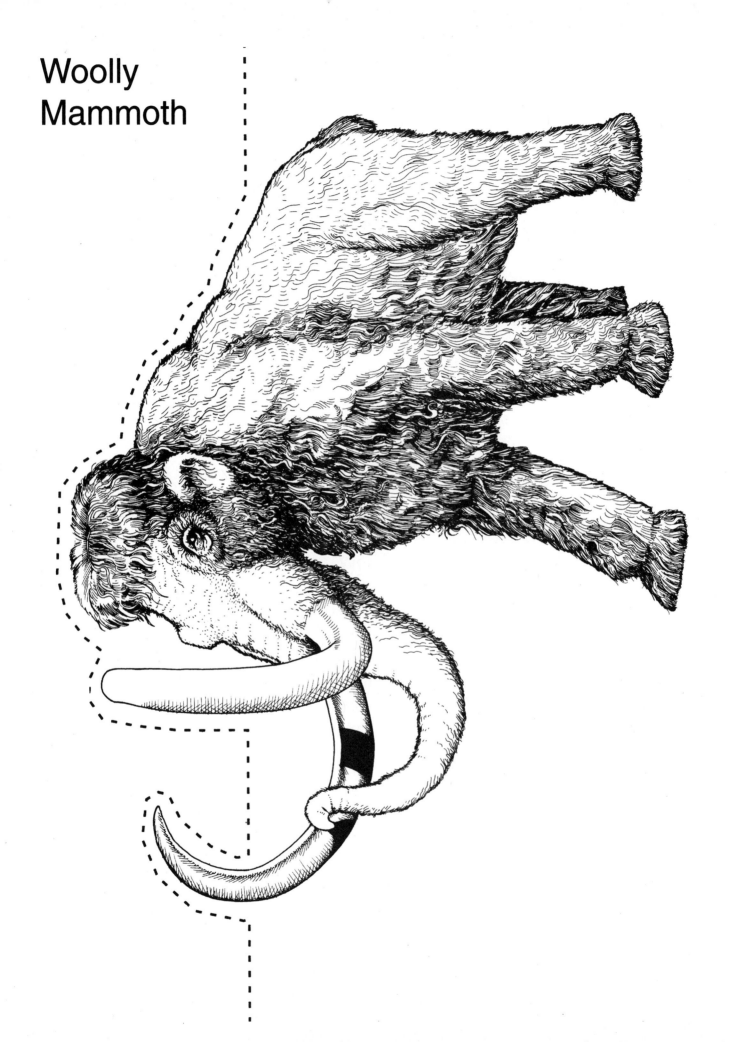

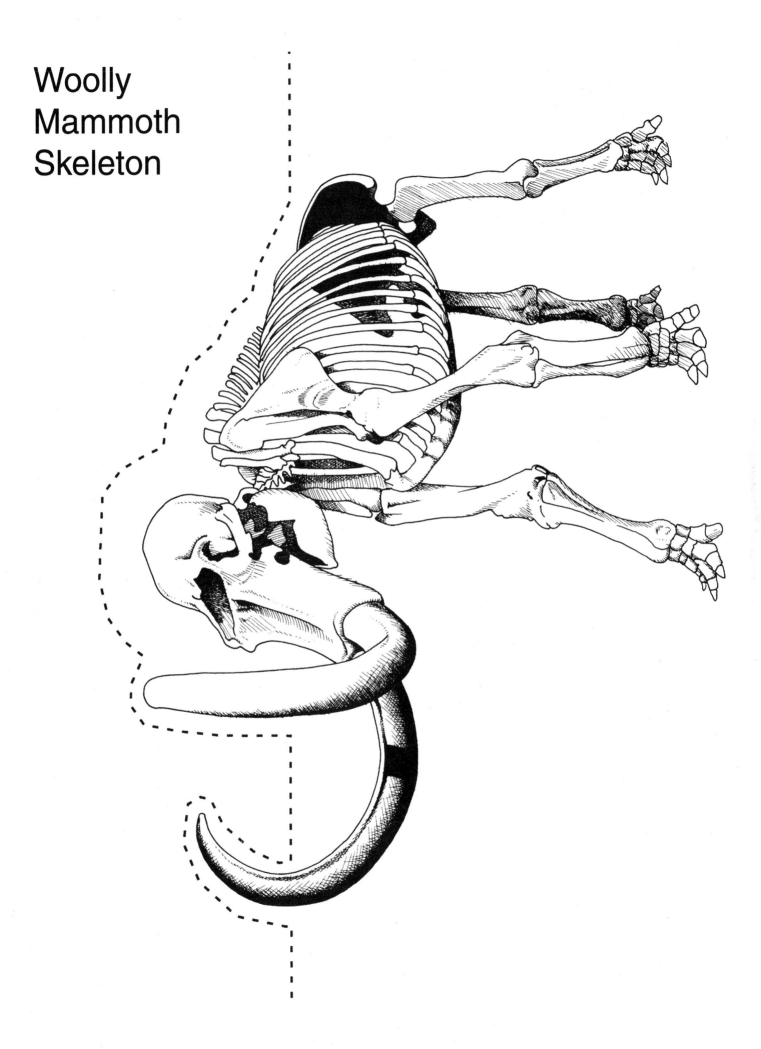

Woolly
Mammoth
Skeleton

Simple Science Report
SABER-TOOTHED TIGER

Provide books and other materials about the saber-toothed tiger for students reporting on this prehistoric animal. (You may need to read these to younger students.) Discuss the information they have learned, then assign a writing task.

> **Saber-Toothed Tiger and Other Ice Age Mammals** by Joanna Cole; Morrow, 1977
> **Saber-Toothed Tiger** by John Duggleby; Honey Bear Books, 1994

Discussion Starters

How would you describe a saber-toothed tiger?

How do you think the saber-toothed tiger caught its food?

Which animal living today is most like the saber-toothed tiger?

Why did you choose this animal?

Skeleton Discussion Starter

Look at the skeleton of the saber-toothed tiger. Can you tell by looking at this skeleton whether the saber-toothed tiger was a meat-eater or a plant-eater? What clue did you use?

Writing Ideas

1. A Report about a Saber-Toothed Tiger
   a. Tell what a saber-toothed tiger looked like.
   b. Tell what a saber-toothed tiger ate.
   c. Tell how a saber-toothed tiger caught its food.

2. Compare the saber-toothed tiger with a modern tiger. How are they alike? How are they different?

3. The saber-toothed tiger was a carnivore. That means it ate meat.
   List all of the animals you can think of that eat meat.
   Circle the names of the carnivores that belong to the "cat" family.

4. Write a story about a saber-toothed tiger.

> **How to Escape from a Saber-Toothed Tiger**
> **Tiger with a Tusk Ache**
> **If I Had Teeth Like Sabers**

Saber-Toothed Tiger

The saber-toothed tiger was a mammal. It was very similar to the large cats such as lions and tigers that are living today.

Saber-toothed tigers lived long, long ago until late in the Ice Age. They did not live as far back as the dinosaurs. After the dinosaurs died out, mammals no longer had to stay small and out of sight. New kinds such as the saber-toothed tiger developed.

Saber-toothed tigers were carnivores. That is, they were meat-eaters. They had teeth like daggers. They would creep up and surprise their prey and kill it quickly with one bite from their long canine teeth. The teeth had jagged edges, kind of like the edge of a bread knife. This made it easier for the teeth to cut into their prey.

The fossils of saber-toothed tigers have been in North America and in Europe.

Saber-Toothed Tiger

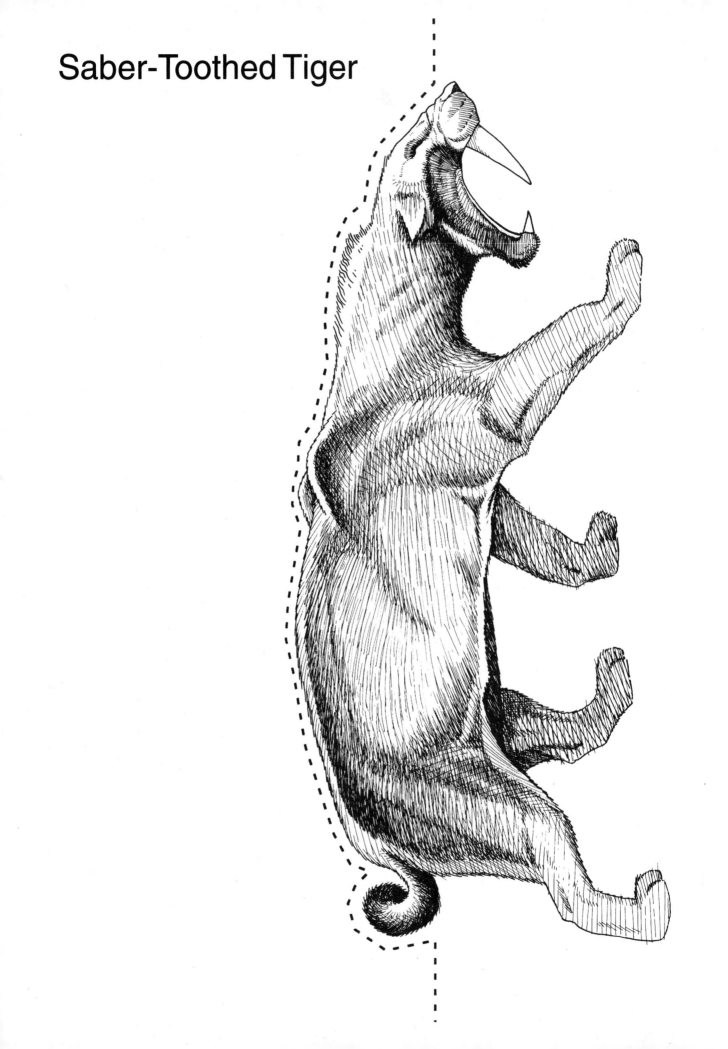

Saber-Toothed
Tiger Skeleton

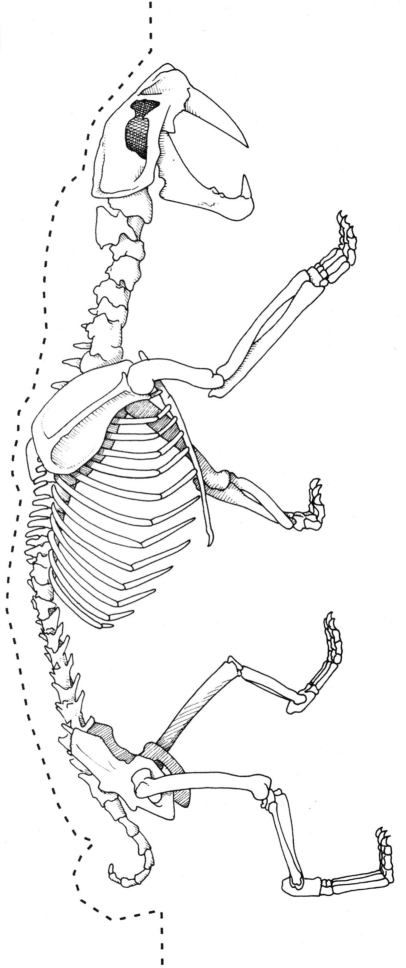

Simple Science Report
PTERANODON

Provide books and other materials about the pteranodon for students reporting on this animal. (You may need to read these to younger students.) Discuss the information they have learned, then assign a writing task.

Pteranodon by Ron Wilson; Rourke Enterprises, 1984

Discussion Starters

How would you describe a pteranodon?

Was pteranodon a dinosaur?

Why was pteranodon able to fly?

Skeleton Discussion Starter

Look at the skeleton of a pteranodon.
What parts of the skeleton show why pteranodon could fly?

Writing Ideas

1. A Report about a Pteranodon
   a. Tell what a pteranodon looked like.
   b. Tell what a pteranodon ate.
   c. Tell how a pteranodon got its food.
   d. Tell how a pteranodon moved.

2. Compare pteranodon and archaeopteryx. (Read about archaeopteryx on page 98.)

3. Explain what you think the large crest on the pteranodon's head was used for.

4. Write a story about a pteranodon.

My Ride on a Pteranodon
When Dinosaurs Took Flight
Pteranodon Goes Fishing

Pteranodon

Pteranodon was not a dinosaur. It was a type of animal called a Pterosaur, a flying reptile. It was the largest animal that has ever flown on the earth.

Pteranodon's body was about the size of a turkey. This little body had a wing span of 27 feet (8.2 meters). Its head was 6 feet (1.8 meters) long from the tip of its beak to the end of its long, bony head crest. It didn't weigh much because of its skeleton of hollow bones. Pteranodon had claws on its back legs. These claws were used to hang onto cliffs and rocky ledges.

Pteranodon was a fish-eater. It had a long beak with no teeth. It used the beak to grab fish as it glided over the surface of the water.

The large head crest may have been used as a brake for landing, or as a rudder since the pteranodon didn't have a tail; or it might have been a balance for the very large beak.

Pteranodon probably used the air currents over the ocean to glide long distances as it searched for food.

Pteranodon fossils have been found in the state of Kansas in the U.S.A.

Pteranodon

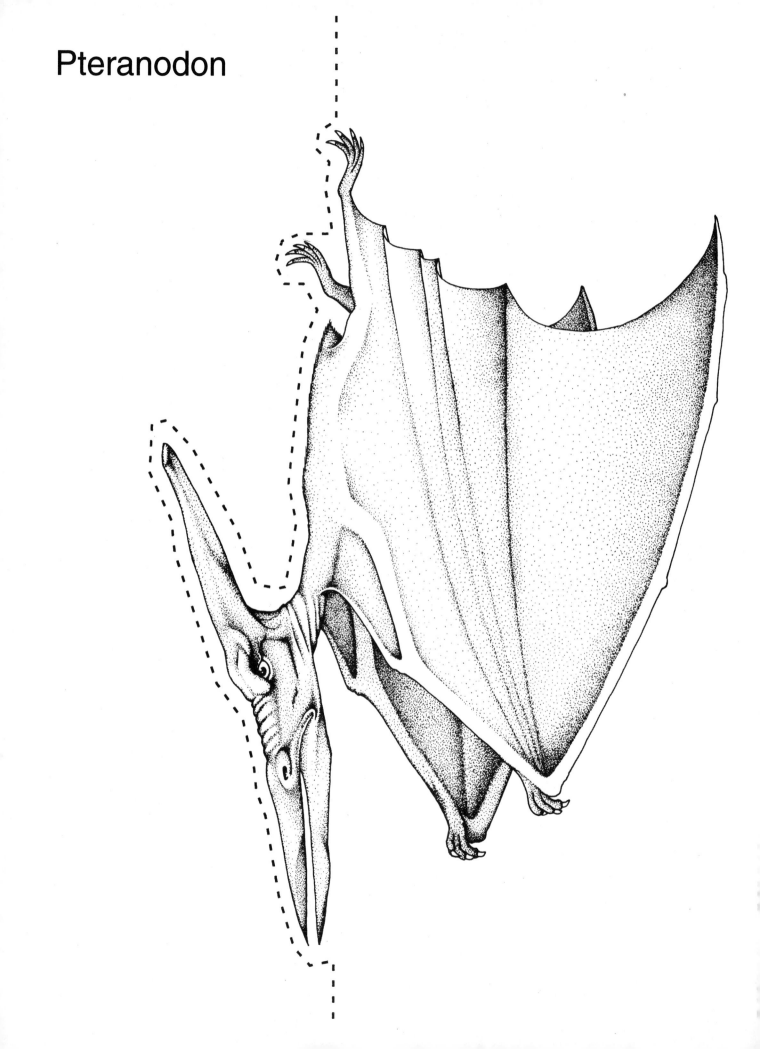

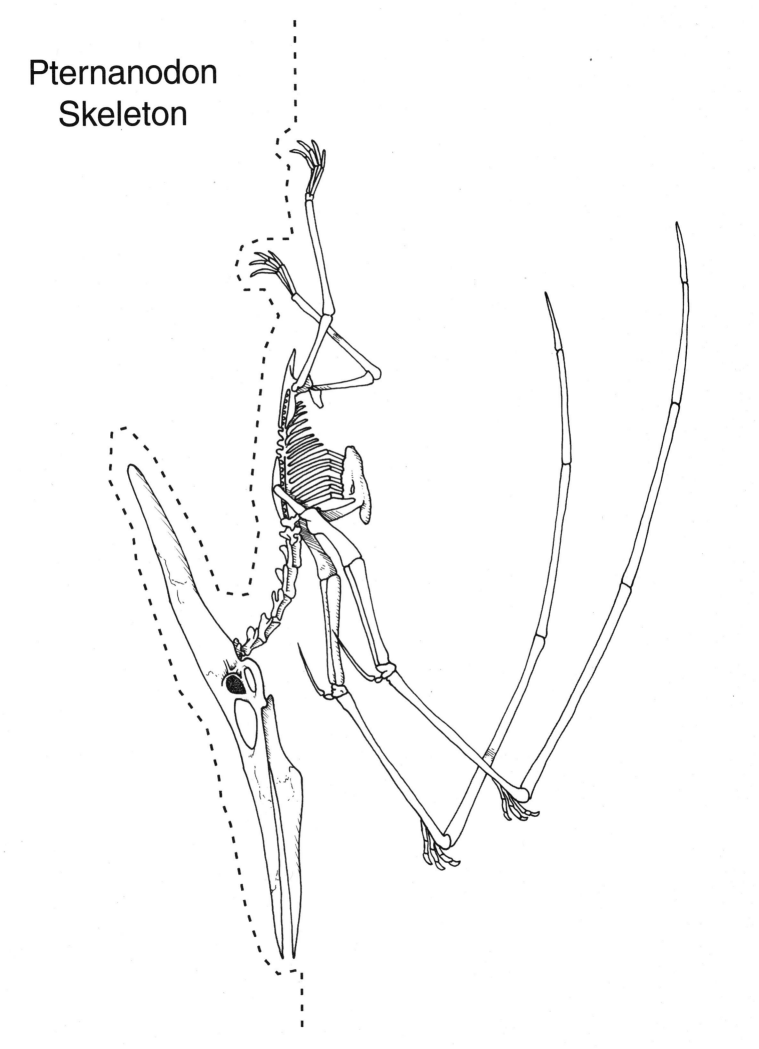

Pternanodon
Skeleton

Simple Science Report

EOHIPPUS

Provide books and other materials about eohippus for students reporting on this prehistoric animal. (You may need to read these to younger students.) Discuss the information they have learned, then assign a writing task.

Discussion Starters

How would you describe eohippus?

What did eohippus eat?

What modern animal is eohippus most like?

Why do you think so?

Skeleton Discussion Starter

Look at the skeleton of eohippus. Look closely at its feet.
Describe how it probably walked.

Writing Ideas

1. A Report about an Eohippus
   a. Tell what eohippus looked like.
   b. Tell what eohippus ate.
   c. Tell how eohippus moved.

2. Compare ancient eohippus and a modern horse. How are they alike? How are they different?

3. How do you think scientists know that eohippus is the ancestor to modern horses?

4. Write a story about an eohippus.

How to Train an Eohippus
Little Eohippus' Escape from Danger
If Eohippus Was Alive Today

Eohippus

The first real mammals lived about 70 million years ago. They were small animals. Many were as small as a modern rat. Eohippus was one of these early mammals. It was about the size of a fox.

Eohippus was the first horse. It didn't look much like a modern horse. In fact, it probably looked more like a dog than a horse. It had a short, thick neck. Besides being very small, it had toes on its feet instead of hooves. Eohippus lived in woodland areas. The toes could spread apart when it took a step and keep it from sinking into the soft ground.

It ate fruits, berries, and leaves. Its teeth were good for biting and crushing soft plants.

As millions of years passed, horses changed. Their legs grew longer and they began to stand on the middle toe of each foot. On modern horses these middle toes have become the horse's hooves.

Eohippus

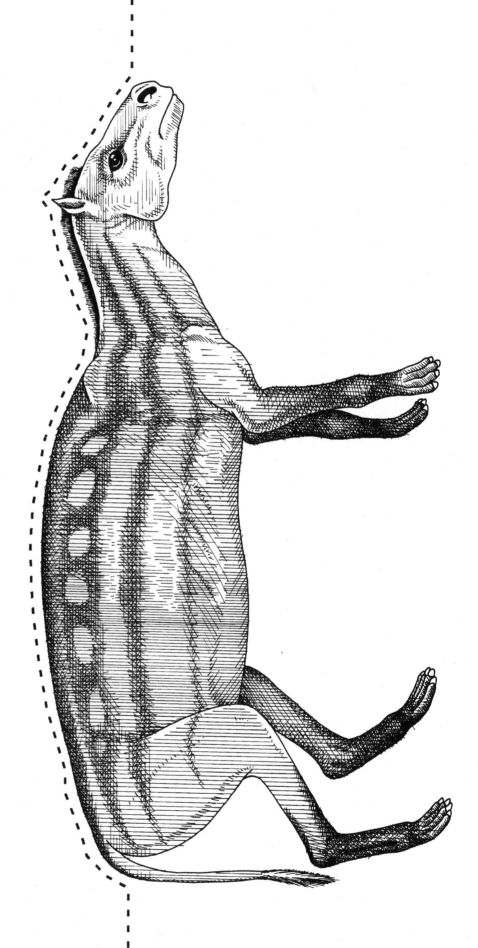

Eohippus
Skeleton

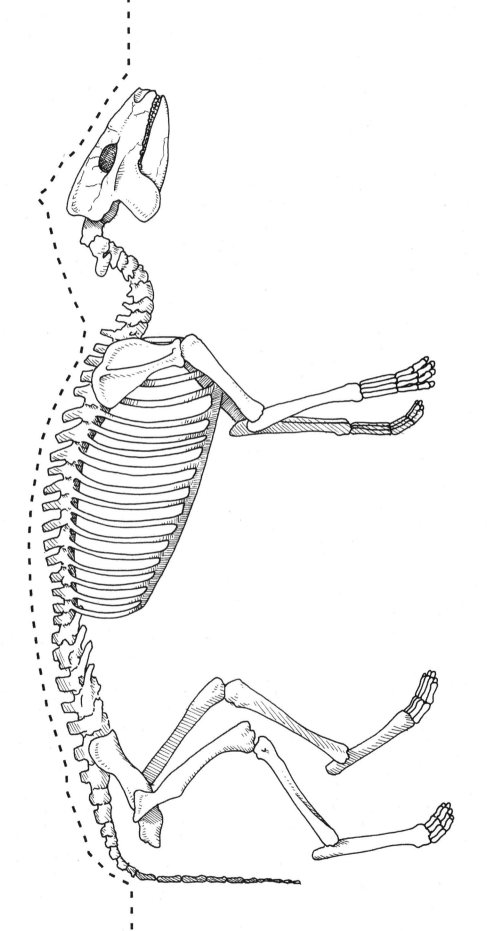

Simple Science Report
PROTOCERATOPS

Provide books and other materials about the protoceratops for students reporting on this dinosaur. (You may need to read these to younger students.) Discuss the information they have learned, then assign a writing task.

Protoceratops by Rupert Oliver; Rourke Enterprises, 1986

Discussion Starters:

How would you describe protoceratops?

Did protoceratops have live babies or lay eggs? How do scientists know?

How was protoceratops like triceratops?

Skeleton Discussion Starter

Look at the skeleton of a protoceratops. Check the teeth.
Do they give you a clue as to what this dinosaur ate?

Writing Ideas:

1. A Report about a Protoceratops
    a. Tell what a protoceratops looked like.
    b. Tell what a protoceratops ate.
    c. Tell how a protoceratops got its food.

2. Describe how the protoceratops was able to protect itself from larger, hungry predators.

3. Describe protoceratops' nest and eggs. Explain how scientists know about these.

4. Write a story about a protoceratops:

   Building a Nest
   Dinner With Protoceratops
   The Mysterious Egg

Protoceratops

Protoceratops was the size of a large pig. It was about 6 feet (1.8 meters) long and very heavy. It probably couldn't run very fast. But it did have some means of protection from larger, meat-eating dinosaurs. Its body was covered in bony armor. It was also small enough to hide in the bushes if danger was near.

Protoceratops walked on four sturdy legs. It had a small frill on the back of its head. It was one of the plant-eating dinosaurs. It had a turtle-like beak which was good for eating tough plants. It had sharp teeth for tearing leaves. It had strong jaw muscles for chewing the tough leaves.

The protoceratops was the first dinosaur in which scientists found fossils of every stage of its life. Potato-shaped eggs have been found laying in bowl-shaped nests dug in the sand. The eggs were laid in two or three circles inside the nest. There were also "hatchling" fossils and fossils of adult dinosaurs in the same area. These fossils were found in Mongolia.

Protoceratops

Protoceratops
Skeleton

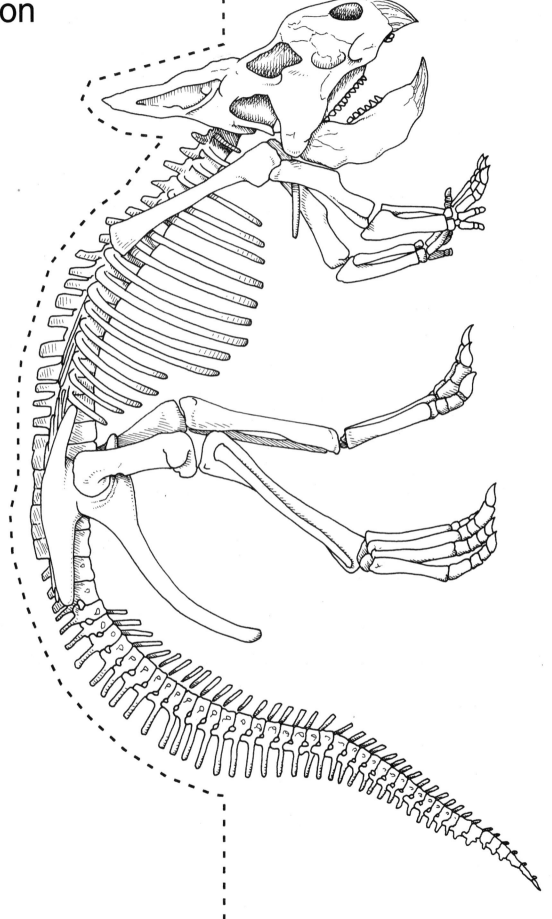

Simple Science Report
TRICERATOPS

Provide books and other materials about the triceratops for students reporting on this dinosaur. (You may need to read these to younger students.) Discuss the information they have learned, then assign a writing task.

Triceratops by William Lindsay; Dorling Kindersley, 1993
Triceratops by Angela Royston; Ray Rourke Publishing Co., 1981

Discussion Starters

How would you describe triceratops?

Why did triceratops need a short, strong neck and a bony collar?

What did triceratops eat?

How did it get its food?

Skeleton Discussion Starter

Look at the skeleton of the triceratops. "Tri" means three.
Can you find the three bones on triceratops' skull?
What do you think these bones were used for?

Writing Ideas:

1. A Report about a Triceratops
   a. Tell what a triceratops looked like.
   b. Tell what triceratops ate.
   c. Tell how triceratops got its food.

2. Describe a day in the life of a plant-eating triceratops. Where would it go? What would it do? What dangers might it face?

3. The "tri" part of triceratops means three. Think of things you know that have "tri" as part of the name. Make a list of these words: triceratops, triangle, tricycle, triathalon, etc.

4. Write a story about a triceratops.

I Woke Up this Morning with Three Horns on My Head
Triceratops and His/Her Musical Horn
Look Out! There's a Meat-Eater around the Corner

Triceratops

Triceratops was one of the dinosaurs with horns. In fact, its name means "three-horned face."

Triceratops was the largest and the heaviest of the horned dinosaurs. It weighed about 5 tons (4.5 metric tons) and was over 25 feet (7.5 meters) long.

Triceratops was a four-legged plant-eater. It browsed the plains looking for food. It had a turtle-like beak and scissor-like teeth. It could snip off tree branches with its sharp beak and chop them up with scissor-like teeth.

It had a smooth, solid neck shield and three horns. One was a short, thick nose horn. Two were enormous 40-inch (102 centimeter) -long, curved horns pointing forward from above the dinosaur's eyes.

This large dinosaur had no real enemies. The horns, frill, and tough, leathery skin made it well-protected.

Triceratops fossils have been found in the states of Montana and Wyoming in the U.S.A. and in Alberta and British Columbia in Canada.

Simple Science Reports

Triceratops

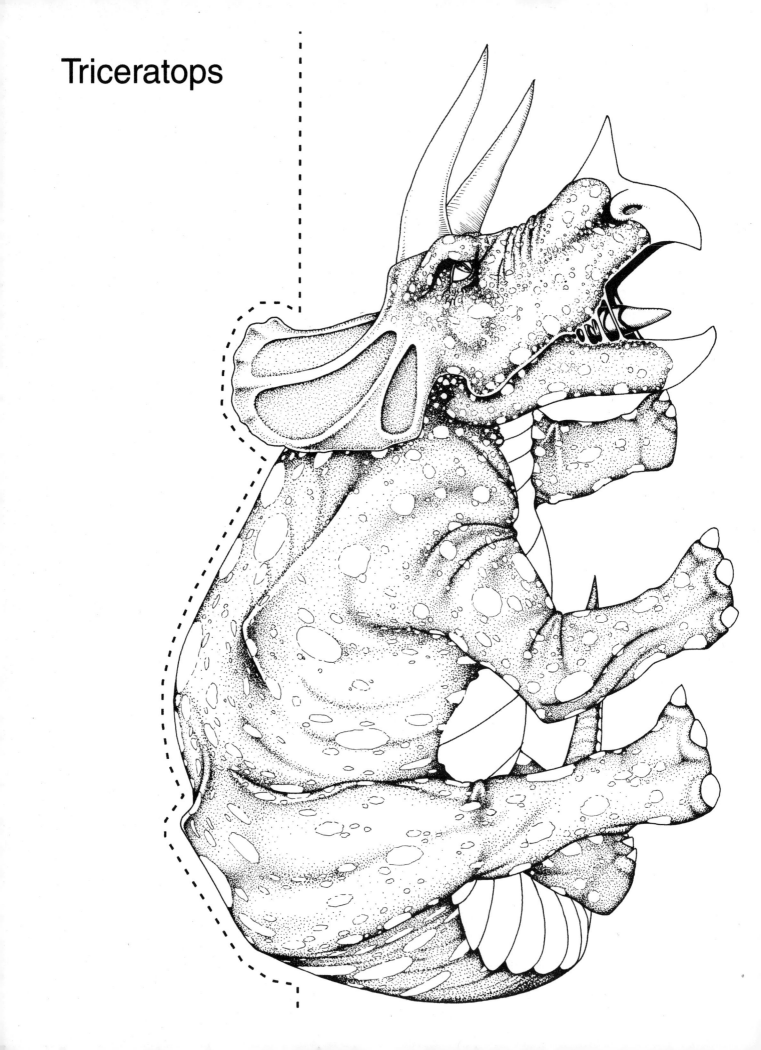